THE PLAY'S THE THING
Teachers' Roles in Children's Play

Elizabeth Jones
Gretchen Reynolds

Teachers College, Columbia University
New York and London

Published by Teachers College Press, 1234 Amsterdam Avenue,
New York, NY 10027

Library of Congress Cataloging-in-Publication Data

Jones, Elizabeth, 1930–
    The play's the thing : teachers' roles in children's play /
Elizabeth Jones, Gretchen Reynolds.
        p.   cm. — (Early childhood education series)
    Includes bibliographical references (p.   ) and index.
    ISBN 0-8077-3171-4 (pbk. : alk. paper)
        1. Play—United States.   2. Education, Preschool—United States.
    3. Teaching.   I. Reynolds, Gretchen.   II. Title.   III. Series.
LB1140.35.P55J66   1992
    372.11′02—dc20   91-46413

Printed on acid-free paper

Manufactured in the United States of America

10   10   11   12   13   14

EARLY CHILDHOOD EDUCATION SERIES
Leslie R. Williams, Editor
Millie Almy, Senior Advisor

ADVISORY BOARD: **Barbara T. Bowman, Harriet K. Cuffaro, Stephanie Feeney, Doris Pronin Fromberg, Celia Genishi, Dominic F. Gullo, Alice Sterling Honig, Elizabeth Jones, Gwen Morgan, David Weikert**

(Continued)

Contents

Foreword

Are you disappointed in your ability to promote play, uneasy about the play that does occur, frustrated by your ineffectiveness in responding to play, or exasperated at the low value others attach to it? If you answer "Yes" to any of these questions, this is the book for you. The authors are skillful observers of play, and chapter by chapter they show aspects of play that only those who have watched long and carefully can describe.

My friend, Ruth Pearce, talks about play as "a bubble of illusion." I have always liked this phrase because it captures the way in which play comes and goes. It can be so brief that it is scarcely noticed before it disappears, or it can be sturdy and complex with other bubbles attached to it. And since it is pretend, once it vanishes ordinary reality takes its place.

To view play as a bubble also describes the empty space within the bubble where the player as creator places the drama. Within this bubble those things that are forbidden or hopeless in the real world can be pretended. Young children pretend at being adults or at being so powerful that even adults must do their bidding. As the creator of these invented plots, a child experiences personal power. With luck there are also friends to share in these fantasies. It is the wish for both the play and the friendship to continue that makes children willing to give up absolute power and work at compromise.

This empty space also gives the player time to find connections between personal experience and perceptions and the outside world with its rules, expectations, and conventions. Within the bubble of play, the player can tinker with these outside constraints and in the tinkering find ways to keep feelings of initiative and uniqueness intact. Thus logic and motivation become aligned to face together the task of mastering the tools of the culture that schooling will demand. The stories in this book will remind you time and again of the profoundly inventive ways in which children work to make these connections, and since play is self-chosen you will see how children reveal much about themselves.

In my mind play is intimately concerned with boundaries. How do we know certain behaviors are "play"? How do we redefine a situation to turn it into play? These distinctions can be difficult for the mentally ill or for those stepping into a foreign culture. Adults who cannot enter into a playful context often create misery for themselves and others. To play requires great flexibility in thinking, an ability to shift context and to add new ideas. These skills, which will be useful across an entire life cycle, do not come without practice.

When children were reared by mothers who were not employed outside the home, there was scant reason to pay attention to play. It occurred without much planning and was welcomed by adults who could then attend to their own concerns. The typical home was stocked not only with toys, but with a variety of loose parts. There were often older and younger children to introduce novelty, and there were private spaces where children could play without interruption. Adults, though busy with other concerns, were available to be watched or questioned, or to settle conflicts. At lunch or during other routines of care, the play of the morning could be discussed. Thus, the roles described in this book occurred in many homes naturally and without reflection. The behaviors of both parents and children were so embedded in the setting that they became invisible and hence unimportant. Today as more and more childhood time is spent in a group setting, it has become essential to recreate an experience that once occurred naturally, and hopefully to offer this experience to children who in the past did not have supports for play. In order to do this the ecology of play and the role of the adult in fostering it must be examined.

The one thing that I like best about this book is that, for me, it describes the knowledge that is required to foster play and to use it as a solid foundation on which to build learning. As these stories unfold, you will see the possibilities for adults to behave in ways that keep the bubble of play from popping prematurely. To do this often requires that the adult create safe boundaries, both visible, in setting up the environment, and invisible, in using adult logic to create transformations and to attach meaning. I suggest that the chapter titles outline a job description that communicates the high levels of professional skill required of those who work with young children. Perhaps this book tells even more about professional development than about play.

Elizabeth Prescott

Introduction

During many years' involvement with programs for young children, we have been participants in and observers of a variety of adult interactions with children at play. In the last 2 years, as members of a resource support team working with preschool staff in programs sponsored by the Pasadena Unified School District and Pacific Oaks College and Children's School, under the auspices of a public-private Partnership Project supported by the Ford Foundation, we have enjoyed the opportunity for intensive observation and for fruitful dialogue with teaching staff. We appreciate the contributions they have made to our thinking and to our collection of stories of children at play. The views expressed throughout the book are our own; they do not represent the Project.

Many of the stories in this book come from our experience in this project. Both to offer continuity to readers and to maintain the privacy of project participants, we tell most of the stories as if they happened at either of two composite settings that have no real-life counterpart: Live Oak Child Development Center and Second Street School. These settings are described below. Teachers who are especially likely to recognize some of our stories, even in these composite settings, are Beni Campbell, Jackie Cotton, Erin Sumner, Jackie McMurray, Connie Wortham, Suzanne Jones, Kathy Reisig, and aide Caridad Bonilla, Pasadena; and Wanda Magiera, San Jose, California. In addition, we have included observations made by some members of the voluntary network of teacher-researchers who received, and contributed to, our project newsletter. We are grateful to Pasadena teachers Theresa Barrios and Georgina Villarino, Madison Preschool; Sandra Rangel and aide Irma Stone, Jefferson Preschool; and Sue Bush and Joyce Mortara, Willard Children's Center; as well as to Linda Torgerson, Juneau Cooperative Preschool, Juneau, Alaska; Gaye Gronlund, Buckeye School District, Redding, California; Anne Solomon, Rocklin School District, California; Joan Newcomb, The Little School, Bellevue, Washington; and Jamie Solow, observer in project preschools. Where a "visitor" or "observer" appears in a story, that's one of us.

SETTINGS

Live Oak Child Development Center is located on a community college campus and serves as a laboratory for early childhood education students. Its half-day preschool combines 3- and 4-year-olds; it is taught by a master teacher with varying numbers of student assistants. The campus child care center is adjacent. Its regular staff is also supplemented by students, and the 3- and 4-year-olds are together.

The children in both programs are racially and ethnically diverse. Those in the preschool come largely from professional families and include a number of faculty children. The child care center serves a socioeconomically mixed population, enrolling children of students, college staff, and, when space is available, faculty.

In the preschool, the master teacher has a master's degree in early childhood education (ECE) and faculty status at the college. Student assistance on a rotating schedule typically provides at least a 1:5 ratio of adults for the 20 children enrolled.

The child care staff includes two bachelor's degree-level head teachers whose schedules overlap, and two paid 6-hour assistants who are typically enrolled part time in the ECE program of the college. Additional student assistants help to maintain at least a 1:8 ratio most of the time. The 24 children have free choice together, both indoors and out, and are divided into smaller "family groups" for other activities.

The separation at Live Oak of the preschool and the child care center reflects the history of their founding and their funding. The same is true for the second setting, described below.

Second Street School is a large public elementary school whose early childhood unit includes a child care center, two preschool classes, and four kindergartens. The child care center has two classes, one of 3-year-olds and one of 4-year-olds. Each class has a teacher and an aide.

The 3- and 4-year-olds in preschool have two separate mixed-age classrooms and share the outdoor space. Each has a teacher and an aide.

The preschool and child care programs at Second Street, which is located in a predominantly African-American and Latino neighborhood, are funded as "compensatory education" and limit enrollment to low-income families. Spanish is the first language of some of the children, and two of the four teachers are bilingual. Each class can accommodate a maximum of 18 children (though the preschool is sometimes underenrolled) with a teacher and an aide. The teachers must meet state certification requirements for preschool—an associate degree in

ECE, or a B.A. in any field with a Child Development Associate (CDA) credential or 24 units in ECE. The on-site early childhood unit director, who supervises the eight classrooms for 3- to 5-year-olds, is elementary-certified with an ECE endorsement. Parent volunteers are sometimes present in the preschool.

The real programs identified by name in this book, Madison, Jefferson, and Willard, are comparable to Second Street preschool. Little Friends (not its real name), which is described briefly in Chapter 2, is a child care center in an urban church.

WHY PLAY?

As preschool educators we have our roots in the developmental approaches of Bank Street and Pacific Oaks, colleges/children's schools whose early childhood traditions predate the influence of Piaget's theory of cognitive development. Along the way, we have been caught up in the new ideas and purposes influencing early childhood education since the 1960s, and we have taught kindergarten and primary grades to add to our preschool experiences. Most recently our sustained contact with a cognitive developmental program—the High/Scope curriculum as implemented in the preschools and child care centers of the Pasadena schools—has challenged us to re-examine yet again our views of what's basic in early childhood education. We are grateful to Joyce Robinson for her active role in this dialogue.

Both the interactionist (Franklin & Biber, 1977) and cognitive interpretations of developmental theory emphasize play—autonomous choice of activity—as the primary mode in which young children construct their understanding of the world. This emphasis on play differs significantly from that of cultural transmission theorists (described in DeVries & Kohlberg, 1990; Franklin & Biber, 1977), who regard play as respite from direct instruction, the appropriate mode of teaching. The latter view, based in behaviorist psychology, dominates elementary education. During the 1960s it gained new influence in preschool education as well, with its inclusion among the nationally adopted models for the newly created Head Start program. With future school success as their objective, behaviorists asserted that poor children must work hard to "catch up"; they don't have time for play (Bereiter & Engelmann, 1966).

Piagetian theory also gained new influence through Head Start models, which took a fairly simplistic view of the theory's educational implications (DeVries & Kohlberg, 1990) but which did provide time for play. Piaget's constructivism, as we have come to understand it, is a powerful rationale for the essential role of play in both cognitive and moral development. It supplements our long-standing awareness of the role of play in socio-emotional development and enables us to be more articulate in our advocacy of play. Most recently, it has supported the extension of advocacy for play into primary education (Bredekamp, 1987; Kamii, 1985a; Katz & Chard, 1989; Wasserman, 1990). It's pleasant to find ourselves no longer paddling in a backwater but riding a new wave of lively and widespread interest in children's play and its place in schools.

TEACHER ROLES

The teacher roles described in this book reflect both our theoretical views of what is desirable and our recent practical experience with what is possible. Working with teachers in the field, we have found that some roles are more readily accepted than others. In this sample of preschool programs, the role of stage manager is the most familiar to all the teachers; without exception, the indoor environments are beautifully provisioned for play. When we began the project, the outdoor environments varied greatly in quality. The idea of outdoor stage management came as no great novelty, however, and teachers have generally been enthusiastic about expanding their definition of this role.

Teacher as planner is another familiar role, although planning for play is less familiar than planning for directed group activities. In our work with teachers, we have continually observed, and communicated to them about, children's sociodramatic play and language, in order to emphasize the value we place on these behaviors in the developmental sequence. Some teachers, especially those inclined to be playful themselves, have increasingly explored the process of planning for play. A number have responded to the idea of providing for literacy as a play script.

The role of teacher as scribe, although a new idea to most of the project participants, has also been greeted with interest. In nearly every classroom, adults are writing down children's words and posting them on classroom walls. Teachers seem to like being "people who write down children's words."

Teacher as teller, a role not on our recommended list, is a traditional role clung to by many adults who work with children. When telling becomes part of mediation or of adult play with children, it typically interrupts play. Teacher as mediator—someone who helps children find their own solutions rather than imposing an adult solution—appears to be a relatively unfamiliar role, though we have seen many examples of its skillful use by a limited number of teachers.

We keep thinking about the role of teacher as player. It is one that both of us, teaching preschool, have moved into naturally, and so our first inclination is to assume that others should too. As observers, however, we have seen a range of teacher involvement with children at play—some supportive and genuinely playful, some intrusive. We have observed teachers who regularly interact with children at play but fail to support the integrity of the play. Their comments and questions come from their preconceived lesson plans; typically, such questions serve to interrupt the play unless children are able to ignore them.

Most "lesson plans" identify learning objectives that are dependent on teaching, not on children's spontaneous learning through play. Yet Kamii's (1985b) studies of children "reinventing" arithmetic through their play with appropriate materials demonstrate the ways in which learning takes place without direct teaching. Kamii has also described how anxious primary teachers are likely to become if they are not teaching arithmetic facts.

Similarly, some teachers of younger children become anxious if they are not teaching shapes and colors, even though these properties appear repeatedly in the play materials in a well-provisioned environment and will be spontaneously used as logical categories by playing children. When we encourage teachers to plan for children's learning through play, we sometimes encounter resistance. Trust in children as learners is even less easily acquired than trust in oneself as teacher, it appears.

For this reason we continue to look for ways to emphasize the crucial roles of assessor and communicator. In these roles teachers become able to convince themselves, as well as others, that the children really are learning as they play.

This book begins in Chapter 1 with the ideas about play that we have constructed in order to remind ourselves, and others, of the importance of children's play. The first three sections include no stories, no conversations, "'and what is the use of a book,' thought Alice, 'without pictures or conversations?'" (Carroll, 1899/1979, p. 1). You will, however, encounter a conversation in the section on "Master Players," and from then on they'll start to come "thick and fast," in Carroll's words. Children's play is full of pictures and conversations. We invite readers to share some of those we've observed and listened to.

THE PLAY'S THE THING
Teachers' Roles in Children's Play

1 Understanding and Supporting Children's Play

To become a master player is the height of developmental achievement for children ages 3 to 5. Master players are skilled at representing their experiences symbolically in self-initiated improvisational drama. Sometimes alone, sometimes in collaboration with others, they play out their fantasies and the events of their daily lives. Through pretend play young children consolidate their understanding of the world, their language, and their social skills. The skillful teacher of young children is one who makes such play possible and helps children keep getting better at it.

Many people working with young children, however, have quite a different view of what teachers do: Teachers teach. They sit children in circles, lead finger plays, and talk about the calendar. They tell children the rules for using the slide and for avoiding collisions with the tricycles. When we watch children playing "school," they play stern teachers who give information, enforce discipline, and issue directives. In the school game as played by both children and teachers, there appears to be a consensus that when teachers talk, children learn. How else will they learn right and wrong? How else will they learn colors and shapes and numbers and letters?

Developmental theory, which has had little influence in education beyond early childhood, is quite clear on this point: "To understand is to invent," in Piaget's (1973) words. Young children learn the most important things not by being told but by constructing knowledge for themselves in interaction with the physical world and with other children—and the way they do this is by playing.

STAGES IN PLAY

The play of 3- to 5-year-olds is different from the play of children before age 3, on the one hand, and of primary-age children, on the other. Developmentally appropriate practice in programs for young children (Bredekamp, 1987) implies changing teaching strategies as the developmental tasks of one stage are mastered and children grow into the next stage. It also implies responsiveness to individual differences. Sustained opportunities for self-chosen play provide the most effective way of responding to these differences.

Erik Erikson and Jean Piaget have articulated complementary theories of the stages of children's development. Table 1.1 summarizes these stages and serves as the outline for this chapter, in which we consider both stages in play and stages in representation. With this framework established we move on to look at the content of play—its scripts—and its mastery by children. The chapter concludes with the teacher's question, "But what do I do while they're playing?" which introduces the teachers' roles that this book is all about.

Under Three: Exploration

The child under age 3, says Erikson (1950), faces the challenges of developing first, trust—the ability to connect—and then, autonomy—the ability to separate. Piaget (Peterson & Felton-Collins, 1986) describes this as the sensorimotor stage, when knowing is physical. For mobile toddlers and 2-year-olds, the developmental task is *exploration* of the world through physical action and through the beginnings of oral language. Kept safe by watchful adults, the competent toddler is a vigorous explorer of and with her own body and what it can do, of other people and their reactions, and of the world of interesting things all around. She pokes and dumps and pulls, tastes and smells and strokes whatever she encounters, increasingly adding verbal commentary in order to communicate with others and to reflect her own experiences.

The thoughtful caregiver for the very young provides an environment rich in sensorimotor experiences to be explored (Stallibrass, 1989), mediates to provide safety while teaching problem solving (Gonzalez-Mena & Eyer, 1989; Muhlstein, 1990), models the use of language at a level suitable to the child's understanding, and responds appreciatively to the beginnings of dramatic play. She is, above all, a giver of *care*, of emotional and physical comfort and warmth in relationship.

Three to Five: Play

From ages 3 to 5, says Piaget, the child is "preoperational." Knowing becomes more than sensory, but its logic is constructed by the

TABLE 1.1. A Summary of Developmental Stages

Age	Primary Learning Activity	Focus of Learning	Modes of Representation	Adult Contribution to Representation	Piaget Stages	Erikson Stages
0–2	Exploration	Physical world: direct knowing	Body language (gesture); developing oral language	Models body language and simple oral language	Sensorimotor	Trust and autonomy
3–5	Sociodramatic play	Experienced world: in stories and images	Body language; spontaneous oral language; imaging with materials; dramatic play	Models oral language; makes provision for play and imaging; models simple literacy	Preoperational	Initiative
6–8	Investigation	Experienced world: classified	Body language; spontaneous oral language; structured oral language; imaging with materials; dramatic play; structured dramatization; developing literacy	Models and structures oral language; makes provision for play and imaging; structures dramatization; models and structures literacy	Concrete-operational	Industry

child for himself, in modes quite different from adult logic. Knowing requires spontaneous action, which takes the form of play: the self-initiated re-creation of one's experiences in order to understand (assimilate) them. Erikson describes the developmental task of this stage as the achievement of initiative—the capacity to choose and plan and accomplish for oneself without being immobilized by anxiety.

For both Piaget and Erikson, the developmental task in preschool is *mastery of play*, most particularly constructive, dramatic, and socio-dramatic play. It is in this stage that the child first becomes a competent representer of experience rather than simply a doer of it. Human society and human thought are built on the achievement of *representation*, which makes possible both looking back and looking ahead, rather than simply living in the moment, and communication removed in both place and time, rather than simply face to face. The exploration of the toddler is direct encounter, not representation. But the dramatic play of 4- and 5-year-olds is increasingly sophisticated representation of both real and imagined experiences.

In their representation, preschoolers make use of spontaneous oral language, which they have typically mastered in its basics and which they continue to refine and expand. They supplement speech with body language, using their whole selves to enact the dramas that inform their lives. In their action, they are storytellers—creators of narratives that, as they play together, become the shared mythology of the community of children. Their stories are enriched by props and costumes, just as the stories of older actors are. Like any preliterate people, they rely on, and continue to create, an oral tradition shared in face-to-face encounters. Their knowing is, in Donaldson's (1978) word, *embedded* in their doing.

Simultaneously, given the availability of tools for the purpose, they are creators of images. Opportunities to make one's mark on the world with pencils and pens, crayons and felt markers, paint and chalk, and hands shaping clay and play dough, enable the child to explore, and eventually use in conscious representation, the realm of visual images, which in all cultural traditions complement the spoken word. These "soft" media are balanced by the hardness of wood scraps and tools and glue, blocks and Legos and other construction toys, all of which impose the discipline of learning how to fit them together but can then be used for the child's own re-creation of the buildings, roads, machines, and tools of the larger world. Drawing and building together, children create the shared imagery that makes their community of experience visible.

The teacher of preschool and kindergarten (in some countries, schools for the whole 3 to 5 age span are known as kindergartens) is concerned with children's mastery of play, oral language, and imagery. She provides a rich play environment with time and space for children to be alone and together. To make their togetherness most productive, she mediates and models empathy, language for problem solving, and the divergent thinking essential to negotiation with others who are different from oneself. Through props and ideas shared in conversation and storytelling, she challenges children to complicate their play scripts and expand their repertoire of dramatic themes. She models appropriately complex oral language and begins to model literacy and numeracy as additional modes of representation.

Developmentally, 5-year-olds are still preoperational, learning by doing. When kindergarten is children's first organized group experience, it serves as a benign orientation to the people, place, and materials of the school, and a chance to learn to play together, be considerate of one's peers, and recognize the teacher's authority. Although many children now enter kindergarten with one or several years of group experience behind them, their modes of knowing and doing are still those of 5-year-olds. Kindergarten, for the preschool veteran, is the opportunity to demonstrate and enjoy mastery of play, to experience the peak of success in doing what one does best, to be "a head taller than oneself" in response to the cognitive challenge that play offers children (Vygotsky, 1978). In play, children learn to plan (Reynolds, 1988). In contrast, "academic" kindergartens reflect a deficiency model rather than a competence model, demanding premature practice of what one *doesn't* know how to do.

Six to Eight: Investigation

Mastery of the tasks of each stage is the best possible preparation for the next. Dyson (1989) describes in detail the ways in which the oral language and drawing skills that primary-age children have already attained help them in their efforts to master story writing. A primary classroom in which children are free to talk and draw, as well as write, at writing time enables them to utilize all the skills gained in play as they move into the tasks of the stage whose challenge, in Erikson's words, is the development of *industry* and competence in the eyes of the adult world. Children ages 6, 7, and 8 are, or are becoming, "concrete-operational"; they are able, says Piaget, to use logical (in adult terms) mental operations in the understanding of their hands-on experiences. They are able to generalize beyond the direct evidence of their senses, though not to forgo such evidence and learn through words alone.

In the primary years, children become "serious players," in Wasserman's (1990) phrase. Katz & Chard (1989) and Wasserman have clearly described the ways in which developmentally appropriate curriculum in primary schools engages children's minds by challenging them to think critically about the *investigations* they undertake both in their spontaneous activity and in their action and interaction as serious players at teacher-planned, open-ended activities. Concrete-operational children are ready for the group-conversational conscious reflection on their play that Wasserman calls "debriefing." Unlike preoperational children, they are conscious learners, capable of product—as well as process—orientation. They set standards for themselves and evaluate their learning.

Primary teachers provide a balance between "breathing out"— self-chosen activity in which children continue to consolidate their understandings as they did in preschool—and "breathing in"—teacher-designed challenges that enable children to "uncover" (D. Hawkins, cited in Duckworth, 1987, p. 7) the important concepts in the curriculum (Ashton-Warner, 1963). Teachers model and guide group conversation about shared experiences. Further, they model and guide practice in the use of literacy and numeracy—the basic abstract modes in which people represent experience. In the primary years, children are ready to begin acquiring the disembedded (Donaldson, 1978), decontextualized (Snow, 1983) skills of thinking required for competence in a scientific culture. Ready, that is, if they are solidly grounded in the embedded meanings of the preschool years and are helped to build bridges from one stage to the next (Ashton-Warner, 1963, Delpit, 1986, 1988; Dyson, 1989; Heath, 1983, Johnson, 1987; Jones, 1987).

Beyond Early Childhood: Dialogue

To round out the picture, children beyond early childhood gradually move toward formal operations in those areas of knowing in which they have solid concrete grounding, though the capacity for thinking without concrete referents does not mature in the elementary years. Formal operations move the focus of learning to the world of ideas, in which the primary learning activity is *dialogue*—with other thinkers, with oneself, and with ideas in books and other media. Adolescents who have mastered the tasks of the earlier stages have the grounding they need to cope with reiteration of all the questions they previously encountered in preschool, made newly immediate by the concrete realities of puberty: Who am I? What do I want? What will I do? "There are," in Maria Piers' words (in Paley, 1988, cover), "certain phases in human development that seem characterized by a greater need for free play and daydream or fantasy. Adolescence is one, and preschool age is the other."

Adolescents' music is among the useful props for their daydreaming. For preschoolers, it's play. "Fantasy play is their ever dependable pathway to knowledge and certainty. I pretend, therefore I am. I pretend, therefore I know. I pretend, therefore I am not afraid" (Paley, 1988, p. viii).

STAGES IN REPRESENTATION

Dramatic play is an intermediate stage in the development of *representation*. Representation develops in a sequence that culminates in becoming a writer and reader. Human beings, beginning in early childhood, not only *have* experiences, they *represent* them for purposes of personal reflection and interpersonal communication. Like the life cycle stages, these stages overlap (see Table 1.1), and all modes of representation continue to be used throughout one's life. The later stages are the more abstract, and the primary purpose of schooling has been to ensure the acquisition of the abstract modes of literacy and numeracy. In literate societies, however, children begin the construction of their understanding of literacy long before they are formally taught.

Gesture—body language—is the first mode of representation (Vygotsky, 1978). As the infant reaches for an object, the adult interprets the reach as pointing—a gesture used to communicate—and responds as a receiver of communication. *Talk*, which follows not long after, develops in the same way, as the adult responds to random babbling by interpreting it as communicative language; and the child, made much of, babbles with increasing selectivity.

Play likewise begins as exploration of the physical world. The toddler puts things in and dumps them out, picks up, stacks, and lets go. A cup may elicit the beginnings of make-believe, as the child pretends to drink from it or give a drink to a stuffed toy. As the child continues to master play, a real cup won't be necessary; if she's decided the bear is thirsty, a block or an invisible cup will be sufficient to sustain the play. Children at play are re-creating familiar scripts from their social and emotional lives. Through active representation, they practice the sequences that lead to mastery.

Similarly, they first explore and then make conscious representations with two- and three-dimensional media. Markers and crayons,
paint, clay, wood scraps, and blocks all serve the child in *image-
making*. Scribbles are given names and move toward increasingly
recognizable approximations of the thing represented. Drawing, like
all other early representations, is self-corrected by the child himself as
both his motor skills and his perceptions continue to mature.

Writing evolves as "children discover that people draw not only
things, but speech" (Dyson, 1989, p. 7). Children as young as age 3
both "draw" and "write," identifying some of their scribbles as writing
as they play at making signs, making lists, and writing letters (Harste,
Woodward, & Burke, 1984). Both writing and reading become play
scripts; becoming a reader begins not with decoding, but with the
sequence, learned by watching adult readers, of picking up a book,
turning it right side up, opening it, turning the pages one by one, and
saying remembered words if the book is a familiar one.

Children invent writing in a process very similar to their invention
of talking, if they receive comparable response from adults (Bissex,
1980; Ferreiro & Teberosky, 1982; Harste, Woodward, & Burke, 1984).
Talking begins with babbling; writing begins with scribbling, and so
the provision of varied tools with which to scribble is a necessary part
of the process. Early talkers move from spontaneous babble to conscious imitation of the sounds made by mature talkers; similarly, early
writers move from spontaneous scribbling to conscious imitation of
the print in their environment. The errors made in each case are not
random; they reflect the child's systems of knowledge at that point in
her development. Young children are logical thinkers, though their
logic may not be the adult's; they are investing their energy in constructing a mental world to make the physical world understandable
(Jones, 1990).

Representation, even more than information, is what schools are
about. The "basics" are still reading, writing, and 'rithmetic, and cri-
tiques of schooling typically stem from perceived deficiencies in students' mastery of these skills. These skills should indeed be learned in
schools; they are not, however, well learned outside of meaningful
context. "The current interest in teaching young children such things as
thinking skills, learning strategies, or computer programming reflects a
regression to the idea that thought and content can be treated sepa-
rately. Mental processes are always content-oriented" (Elkind, 1989,
p. 114). While children can be motivated to skill practice by threats
and bribes (otherwise known as rewards and punishments, or positive
and negative reinforcement), they learn most effectively when they

perceive the learning as intrinsically interesting and useful in their lives.

Developmentally appropriate education builds on the intrinsic motivation of the child. In the preschool years, children are highly motivated to play; it is difficult to get them to settle down to "work," as teachers in academic preschools and kindergartens regularly discover. The myth of the short attention span of young children derives from such efforts. Young children are perfectly capable of concentrated effort over extended periods of time if what they're doing is their own idea. Teacher interruption of play for the purpose of teaching abstract concepts and skills contradicts what we know about the learning process for young children.

Play is not the work of the devil, as our Puritan tradition would have us believe. It is the most important activity of early childhood; in play children are at their most competent. Kindergartens, preschools, and child care centers need to be about play if they are to support growth rather than to impede it.

THE CONTENT OF PLAY

Using language, construction with materials, and their own bodies in action, children begin to represent their experiences. They improvise scripts that the observing adult can easily identify and give name to: Morning at Home, Superman, Going to the Store, I'm Driving My Fast Car, Feeding the Babies, Blast Off! The scripts played by the children in a preschool or kindergarten program reflect the convergence of the experience children bring with them and the materials and equipment in the school environment.

A script is a play theme based in the child's real or fantasy experiences. It is the dramatic portrayal of a sequence of events, with predictable variations. Children playing together keep it somewhat unpredictable by adding new ideas and dialogue as they negotiate the emerging script with each other. The "cooking" script may include play behaviors such as taking food from the cupboard or refrigerator, putting it in a pan, turning on the stove, stirring, turning off the stove, putting the food on a plate, putting the plate on the table as part of a table setting, and sitting down to eat. The "baby" script may include the baby's crying, picking up the baby, changing its diapers, warming a bottle, giving the bottle, burping, wrapping the baby in a blanket, taking it out in the stroller, coming home, and putting it to bed. The actor in the "driving" script gets in (on) the car, turns the key, steps on the gas, revs the engine, turns the wheel, speeds up, slows down, jams on the brakes, and may crash! And sometimes scripts are combined as episodes in a continuing saga such as "Cooking for Baby and Taking Her for a Drive."

The familiarity of life's scripts is what makes the daily life of adults efficient. All the steps in the sequence have become second nature, and so we are free to think about other things as we cook or drive. We recognize this only when we find ourselves in an unfamiliar setting—driving a borrowed car, trying to shop in a new supermarket, placing a phone call in a foreign country.

Young children, new in the world as they are, play in order to find their way around in what is for them the foreign country of adults, to master its daily scripts. Into this reality-based play children frequently weave fantasy themes, which give them practice with metaphors useful for representing feelings. Fantasy play enables children to experience power and mastery, to be big in imagination even though they're really little. Even adults use fantasy to compensate for and illuminate the mysteries and frustrations of daily life.

Pretending enables children to represent problems and practice solving them, to ask questions and learn about the world in terms they can understand. Play is self-motivated practice in meaning-making; its themes are repeated over and over until the child is satisfied that she's got *this* figured out. In the process she is acquiring learning strategies, knowledge, and skills. Issues of right and wrong arise as children negotiate with each other and as adults mediate. Shapes, colors, and numbers are embedded in the properties of dishes and blocks, puzzles and paints.

MASTER PLAYERS

Effective teaching of 3- to 5-year-olds is directed toward helping them all become master players. The master player is a child who uses materials imaginatively in sustained, complex dramatic play. He is able to negotiate with others to keep the play going, working out social as well as material problems.

> Two 4-year-olds were involved in this episode for 45 minutes and returned to continue it the next day.
> LAURIE: Let's build an airport.
> TAMARA: We need planes.

LAURIE: Let's make a tower, a big one like the one in the L.A. airport.

TAMARA: We need a lot of cars and a parking lot.

TEACHER: I like what you are making.

LAURIE: It's the airport.

TAMARA: Like the one in L.A.

TEACHER: I see that you have planes, cars, and buildings. Do you see anything else in the airport?

LAURIE: People. Can we use the little people?

TEACHER: Yes.

TAMARA: Bags. We need bags. I know! We can use the small blocks.

LAURIE: We need tickets. My mom had tickets when we went to Washington. (She goes to cut up some papers.)

TAMARA (*when clean-up time is announced*): Teacher, can we save this till tomorrow?

The next day they brought Barbies to school to be the mothers and sisters at the airport. More children joined them. At one point they even had the train going around the airport with people inside.

(Georgina Villarino, teacher/observer)

These are competent 4-year-olds engaged in mastering the process of inventing mutually agreed-upon representations of their experience. They are deciding what to do and how they will play it out. Through playing, they are discovering who they are, what they know, and what they want to learn next. They are practicing communication with peers: Will you play with me, and can we agree on what we're playing? They are also practicing communication with an adult, as a way of asserting themselves and getting their play needs met: Can we improvise with materials, and do you value our play enough to let us continue it tomorrow? They are exercising developmentally appropriate behavior: *initiative*.

The developmental stage of initiative (see Table 1.1) precedes the stage of industry, in which primary-school children face the challenge of becoming competent at tasks whose rules are made by adults. The child can cope more effectively with this task when she has already experienced making up her own rules, creating her own meanings, and discovering who she is and what she knows and cares about. Self-esteem and self-concept are the outcomes of preschool play. Play enables the child to create herself as a conscious human being, unique among all human beings.

BUT WHAT DO I DO WHILE THEY'RE PLAYING?

Many adults who teach young children say they feel at a loss when children are "only playing." Some use play time as a welcome opportunity to chat with other adults or to grab a cup of coffee or to prepare the next teacher-directed lesson. Others are vigilant for children's safety and quick to intervene if anything worries them, but pay little attention to the content of the play and its educational significance for children.

Teacher as Observer

This book is about paying attention to play. It focuses on the importance of play for young children ages 3 to 5 and on the skills a teacher of young children needs to support play. We emphasize that the most fundamental skill is observation, in which teachers of young children ask some of these questions: What is happening for this child in this play? What is his agenda? Does he have the skills and materials he needs to accomplish his intent? To answer these questions, adults need to practice taking the child's perspective, and careful observation of children at play enables one to do just that. Observing, the teacher can try to name the play as the child might name it.

> Becky, a child who typically watches or wanders rather than playing, and who hasn't left behind her anything to be put away, ignores the announcement of clean-up time. After clean-up, she knows, it will be time to sit on the rug with books, so that's where she goes. She sits in front of the block shelves. Instead of picking up a book, she reaches tentatively for a block. She takes out a long block and stands it carefully on its end. It balances. She tries another, and both crash.
>
> TEACHER (*hearing the noise*): Becky, it's not play time now. It's clean-up time. Let's put the blocks away. (She puts them away herself without waiting for Becky's help. Becky says something softly.) What did you say, Becky?
>
> BECKY: I didn't play with the toys.
>
> TEACHER: That's okay, we all help at clean-up time. Can you help Stephanie put the dolls to bed?
>
> She takes a passive Becky by the hand and leads her to the doll corner.

The teacher's name for this incident might be "Becky Isn't Helping." But Becky's name for it might be "What Will Happen If I Do

This?" Becky's question is one regularly asked by scientists; it's a preliminary step to hypothesis testing.

The teacher intervened to impose her rules on Becky's behavior: It's not time to play now. Everyone helps with clean-up. Sensible rules, these. And she was in a hurry, as adults often are. It was, after all, clean-up time. But Becky is a child whose lack of awareness and initiative has been of real concern to the staff, and here she's showing a little initiative, unfortunate though her timing may be.

A teacher who was free to pause and consider Becky's motives might have thought: "She's trying to get out of clean-up. But she didn't play with anything. And now she is playing, when there's no one else in the blocks." The teacher might simply have watched to see what Becky would do next. Or she might have commented, "The blocks fell down. I wonder if you can stand them up again?" Or she might have begun thinking about ways to extend Becky's interest at a more appropriate time, perhaps by providing a protected space to build in. The adult whose priority is observing slows down to match the child's pace, exerting herself not to keep everything orderly but to ask herself the questions, "What is this play about? How could I support it?"

Imposing rules and maintaining order are part of teaching-as-managing. This is teacher behavior we all remember: "Stop talking . . . pass out papers . . . do your homework now . . . time to get in line." Teaching-as-paying-attention is more difficult, more sophisticated, and more in tune with children's interests.

Elementary education typically starts with questions of curriculum and method: What shall we teach the children, and how? Early childhood education has instead emphasized child study: What can we learn from the children, if we observe their naturally occurring behaviors? Piaget's "clinical" observations have supported educators' discoveries that children construct knowledge for themselves through their spontaneous activity. And so, in the early years, teaching is based on observing. This book is full of observations—stories about real children and the adults who work with them as teachers.

Teacher as Doer

Teachers don't, however, only sit and watch play. They also make play possible. This book is organized in terms of the actions adults take to free themselves to observe children at play. Complex dramatic play typically happens when no adult is directly involved—when children are on their own in a thoughtfully planned environment, using skills and exploring interests that adults have helped them to develop.

Teachers of young children take responsibility both for the content of play and the skills—physical and social—that children bring to their play. Through observation, they assess each child's development and plan what choices to make available in support of the continued development of the child's initiative in play. In this process, teachers may act in all of these roles:

Stage manager
Mediator
Player
Scribe
Assessor and communicator
Planner

Each role of the teacher is explored in depth in the chapters that follow. (For a complementary analysis of teachers' roles in children's play, see Van Hoorn, Nourot, Scales, & Alward, in press.) Chapters 2–4 are about the basic roles of stage manager, mediator, and player, which support children directly as they grow toward mastery of play. Behaviors that interrupt play are examined in Chapter 5. The more sophisticated roles of scribe, assessor and communicator, and planner are introduced in Chapters 6–8.

In Chapter 9 we look at teachers' development of skills in implementing the various roles, considered in terms of the practical realities of staffing early childhood programs. Finally, we return to the needs of young children in the modern world, reflecting on ways in which adults can help them build bridges of meaning among the multiple settings in which their lives unfold.

But now, the stage is set, and here comes Jenny.

2 Teacher as Stage Manager

The teacher's contribution to play always begins with the physical environment, with stage setting. Developmentally, physical knowledge comes first. Children need the physical stuff of the world, the "It" out there beyond the "I" and the "Thou" (Hawkins, 1974, p. 48). It's up to adults to provide enough space, enough materials, and enough time, by arranging the environment so the play can happen.

What can I do here today? Young children don't ask this question. They *do* it.

Jenny comes through the gate at Live Oak preschool slowly, clutching her mother's hand. On the low wall near the gate, around the edge of the sandbox, there's a beautiful collection of road-building equipment. Bright yellow dump trucks, bulldozers, and graders are neatly spaced along the wall. What 3-year-old could resist, with all that sand waiting to be dug?

Dulcie can't. She charges through the gate right behind Jenny, spots the bulldozer and grabs it. "Mine!" she announces to the world. She plunks herself down in the sand. She bulldozes straight across the hole Marcos has been carefully digging for 5 minutes. "Hey!" he says, annoyed, and socks her. She socks him back.

The teacher approaches. "Marcos, what do you want to tell Dulcie?" she asks, squatting down between them.

But Jenny isn't interested in bulldozers or sand or arguments over territory. She stands beside her mother sucking her thumb, interested in nothing in particular. Her feelings—Do I really want to be here?—are much more compelling for her than anything in the environment.

"Want to take off your jacket and put it in your cubby?" Jenny's mother asks, hoping that Jenny will see something indoors that she wants to do. Sure enough, right next to the cubbies there's a collection of large rubber animals, sorted into traditional family groups of father, mother, baby, parading along the shelf above the blocks. Jenny forgets about her jacket and even about her thumb. "Look, Mommie, the baby horsie," she says happily. She takes the horse family off the shelf and settles down with them in the blocks. She's building a corral for them as her mother says goodbye.

The staff in this preschool has given a lot of attention to setting the stage for play. For the first hour of the morning, and sometimes longer, children can choose among a variety of activities both indoors and outdoors, when weather permits. Outdoors today there are trucks in the large sand area, paints at two easels, a variety of wheel toys, and a climbing structure with a slide. Indoors the block area has animals and small cars to use with the floor blocks. There are books and stuffed animals in a corner full of pillows, varied manipulatives on the shelves, and play dough, made of flour, salt, water, and rich brown powder paint, on the table. A home corner, partially walled off by shelves, offers child-sized kitchen and bedroom furniture, dress-up clothes both male and female, a variety of grocery items, and interesting collections of cleaning supplies and fix-it tools.

In arranging the environment, the staff has worked hard at clarifying the *figure–ground relationships*.

CLARIFYING FIGURE–GROUND RELATIONSHIPS

Remember the black-and-white drawing that keeps showing up in psychology textbooks in the chapter on perception? If you see the white as figure and the black as ground, it's a vase. If you see the black as figure and the white as ground, it's two profiles looking at each other. Your perception keeps shifting, in an interesting demonstration of the relationship between figure (what you're looking at) and ground (the background against which you see it).

Perceptual skills develop slowly, through repeated experience. For a crawling baby, depth is a new phenomenon; it takes a while to recognize, at the top of the stairs, an edge at which one should stop. On family trips in the car, if the driver suddenly says "See that bird!" the other adults probably will, and the children probably won't; they can't yet shift their focus fast enough. Children, with much less experience, see their world less confidently. And even experienced adults can be confused by unfamiliar configurations, or by drawings designed to confuse.

To play requires the ability to choose. Making choices is easier if the figure–ground relationships are clear. "What can I do today (here in this strange place with all these people and my mommy about to leave)? Oh, I see a horsie. I like horsies. See my horsie, Mommy? . . . 'Bye, Mommy."

Jenny didn't have to look for the baby horse in a toy box or amid a jumble of other animals she hasn't yet learned to love or even to name. The preschool staff had arranged the animals carefully, each in its family group and none close enough to hostile species to risk being bitten. The baby horse was right there with its parents. The arrangement enabled Jenny to focus and made her choice easy. She didn't want lots and lots of animals; she wanted the horse family. And as she took charge of them and began building a safe fence around them, it was all right for her mommy to go. By representation in play of the relationships and feelings in their real lives, children gain a sense of mastery over them. The "macrosphere" of the larger world is beyond their control, but within the "microsphere," the small world they create in their play, they're in charge (Erikson, 1950). It's a safe place to take initiative.

Attentive teachers of young children work on clarifying figure-ground relationships throughout the day, as they support problem solving, ask helpful questions, and pick up scraps of play dough.

> For a while the play dough table is ignored; most of the children are busy outdoors, and those indoors are involved in dramatic play. Finally a group of boys bursts in, superheroes in the midst of a chase. One of them spots the new brown play dough.
>
> "Look, doo-doo!" he exults. The others are quick to follow his lead: "Ka-ka." "Poo-poo." "Ka-ka poo-poo," yells the most imaginative. They crowd around the table. "Is that really poo-poo?" Matthew asks the teacher doubtfully.
>
> "What do you think?" she asks. "How could you find out?"
>
> "Poo-poo stinks! Stinky, stinky poo-poo!" chants Brad. But Matthew ignores Brad; he's really curious. "I don't think you'd put poo-poo on the table," he decides. "I think it's play dough." He sits down and touches it tentatively.
>
> "Yuck! Stinky poo-poo!" yells Brad, trying to keep his fascinating theme going. But he's lost it. The teacher ignores his bathroom talk, and the other children's curiosity and pleasure in play dough take over. Two more boys join Matthew at the table. Brad wanders off, looking for some new action.
>
> Play dough and table knives keep Matthew, Zach, and Warren absorbed for 10 minutes. The conversation turns quickly to cookies and doughnuts. The teacher sits with the boys for a few minutes, then moves on to the other areas.

When she returns, the boys have left; Brad swooped by and enticed them into a superhero chase. They have left the table strewn with the remains of their work. A student observer is sitting nearby, and the teacher sits down at the table to talk with her. As they talk, the teacher absently shapes some bits of play dough into pancakes, making a pile of them. Then she starts rolling up the stray bits of dough, snowball-fashion. Pretty soon there's a whole row of dough balls on the table.

Camilla arrives. "How did you make those?" The teacher demonstrates. Camilla picks up a knife and starts slicing one of the balls into pancakes. Rosie arrives and wants to make pancakes too, but there's only one knife to be found. "Could you use the tortilla press to make pancakes?" the teacher asks, getting it off the shelf. "No pancakes. Tortillas," says Rosie happily. Lots of tortillas.

The teacher is rolling another ball as Brad arrives, out of breath and belligerent. He seems to have forgotten about poo-poo. "What are you doing?" he asks. "I'm making a ball," she replies. He gives her a challenging look, then raises his fist and smashes the ball. She admires his strength and ingenuity, and tells him so: "You made a pancake."

So he did. He reaches for another ball and flattens it too. He wants another, and she shows him how to make one. Now they're both rolling dough around.

Marcos arrives. He takes all the remaining balls to make a snowman. His pile gets so high that he has to squish them onto each other so they won't fall down. Then he puts a pancake hat on top and pulls it down, droopy-mushroom fashion, inviting the teacher to admire it. She does.

This teacher habitually brings order to the environment as she moves through it. Before she gets to the play dough, she has picked up two dolls from the floor and put them back to bed, hung up a fire hat, and spent a few minutes shelving scattered blocks. But her assistant scolds her about picking up blocks: "That's the children's job."

"Yes, it is," the teacher agrees. "They need to help with clean-up. But right now it's still play time, and I want them to be able to see clearly what's here to play with."

"But when you straighten things, the kids just mess them up," objects the assistant.

"I know. That's why I do it," grins the teacher, as she picks bits of old dry dough out of a cookie cutter.

What this teacher does is to keep re-establishing clear figure-ground relationships, spontaneously creating order out of disorder to make the possibilities clear to children. If they "mess up" (use and change) what she has provided, she knows she's succeeded in supporting their play. Their order is always different from hers. And the classroom is theirs, not hers; she sets it up so they can re-create it.

Meeting with her student assistants later in the day, she tries to explain her thinking to them, after Beth has asked, a bit petulantly, "Why do we have to put everything out so neatly when the kids don't have to keep it that way?"

"What I want to do is create a logically ordered presentation of materials that will make sense to the children," the teacher says slowly, choosing her words as she thinks about the question. "If they know where to find things, they can focus their energies on using materials in play."

"But they're messing up the order," protests Noemi. "This morning I must have spent 15 minutes sorting out all the dress-up clothes and putting them where they belong, and you know where they ended up? In a great big jumbled pile in the wagon, in the corner of the yard under the trees. The whole family picked up and moved to Mexico— that was what they were playing—and practically everything from the house corner went along with them. All my work wasted!"

"Hey, but the play was great," says John, who had helped the movers get the wagon out the door and off the porch. "I was taking notes on what they said. The grandparents came to meet them when they got to Mexico and they went straight to a wedding. Those dress-ups did get used, Noemi. Everyone put on all the clothes they could find."

"They messed up your order, Noemi, so they could transform it into their own," says the teacher. "If this were your house, you might choose not to let them do that (though that can be a constant struggle between parents and children at home). But this isn't a home; it's a preschool for children. It's their place, not ours. Our job is to make it work for them.

"When it ends up looking messy, that's usually a sign that we've succeeded—that the children are using the materials abundantly to support their own 'wonderful ideas' [Duckworth, 1987]. The clutter is like that in a chef's kitchen or an artist's studio, left in the wake of the creation of a masterpiece."

"Like my desk!" says John.

"That makes sense," says Beth. "But it turns us into housekeepers, doesn't it? I don't know that I like being a housekeeper."

"I'm a rotten housekeeper at home," says the teacher, "but I have to be a diligent one at preschool or the play deteriorates. It's the adults, not the children, who are responsible for the larger picture, the overall order of the play environment. As the children create new order—a block tower, a painting, play dough tortillas, a doll tucked carefully into bed—the surroundings get cluttered with strewn blocks, a painting left on the easel, scraps of dough, and doll blankets on the floor. So, as you've noticed, while children are playing I do a lot of low-key picking up and putting away.

"You know all the discussions we've had about the differences between open and closed materials? Open materials can be combined and recombined in any number of ways, limited only by the imagination. To make a puzzle, which is closed, the child has to be able to put the pieces together in their right order. But completion of an open task occurs whenever the child is satisfied with the order she has invented.

"At clean-up time, which happens after play time is over, we re-establish our order. The purpose of our order is to help children get started and keep focused in play, both of which depend on the balance between too much complexity and not enough. Were you watching Jenny this morning? For her, the balance offered by the animals in family groups was just right; thank you, John, for setting those up so nicely. She could see the possibilities and get started, which she couldn't have done if they'd all been jumbled in a toy box. And if they'd been pieces in a puzzle, I don't think that would have worked either; Jenny was already anxious about her mom's leaving; she didn't need the anxiety she would feel if she were trying to do a closed task right. Open materials in suggested order—the adults' order that need not be maintained—leave the most room for children to create their own ideas in play."

PROVIDING ENOUGH PROPS

Second Street School has two preschool classes that share a large asphalt play yard with a kindergarten class. Early in the fall, when an observer begins visiting regularly, it's evident that the teachers of all three classes have given thought to the organization of their classrooms, but not as yet to the shared outdoor space.

September
There are thirty 3- and 4-year-olds outdoors. The stationary equipment includes four swings and several climbers and slides. There is a large expanse of sand under the equipment, and a lone frisbee. Children are climbing, sliding, swinging, waiting for turns on

the swings, running, and throwing sand. Four children are playing with the frisbee. Three boys are wrestling in the sand. There is a bike path painted on the asphalt; several children are running around it. A boy discovers that if he uses his heels, the slide makes a fine loud drum, but an adult tells him to stop.

A running child falls and skins her knee. She cries loudly. "Why is she crying?" one adult asks another. "She was running," is the accusing answer.

The observer is uncomfortable, seeing all these children without enough to do to keep them either happy or safe. From her viewpoint, the only imaginative play in the yard, which the observer names Run Away and Hide!, has been organized by two small boys who are hiding in the bushes, then running around the corner and along the covered walkway adjacent to the yard. They are entirely out of sight of any adult. They disappear and reappear; it is some time before they are caught at this illegal game.

By the time children have been outside for 25 minutes, some are asking to go in for lunch. But it isn't lunch time. "I can break down the door," the observer hears one boy say to his suitably impressed friends. Several children waiting on the porch begin a running game until a teacher arrives to organize them into a line and take them in.

Early October

All three classes are outside, for a total of at least 45 children. Teachers have brought out bikes and a hoop. Many children are waiting for turns. Complaints of "Teacher!" are frequently heard. It's been windy, and the porch and the dirt under the trees are covered with leaves.

The observer, back for another visit, foresees another frustrating morning for everyone. Because she's had some chance to get acquainted with the preschool teachers in weekly seminars they've been having together, she decides to risk stepping out of proper observer behavior. "Would it be all right," she asks one of the teachers, "if I brought out a few crates and the animals from the block area in the room?" The teacher, surprised but curious, thinks about the idea and then agrees.

The observer puts the crates on the porch, stands up several animals in a crate, and puts the remaining animals in the leaves under the trees. "What are those for?" asks a curious child. "I thought they might like to come outside in the leaves," says the visitor. "Can we play with them?" the child asks. And play they do—zoo, animal fight, bury animals in the leaves, take them for a bike

ride, wash them in the drinking fountain. Animal-washing is particularly absorbing for several children over a long period of time.

Enterprising children from the other preschool class go into
their room and bring out their animals—and a few cars for good
measure. Oh, oh, the two rooms' animals are going to get mixed up,
thinks the observer. How nice, a cooperative classification activity in
the making, is her second thought. Our animals, your animals. She
suggests the idea to the other teacher. As she leaves, she wonders
what will be happening on her next visit—or whether she'll even be
welcome.

Late October

The observer, apparently welcome, returns to spend some time
in the other preschool room. At the end of circle time the teacher
asks the children, "What would you like to bring outside?" "Animals," says one boy, and they do.

Outdoors, the sand table is filled with bird seed, not sand, and
lots of tools. There is also a crate full of tools that children can take
to the sand around the climbers. There are bikes and wagons, stilts,
a ball, and leaves. The preschool teacher across the way has spread
a gym mat on the porch against the classroom wall, added two lacy
pillows, a quilt, and some dolls to make a large bed, and now is sitting comfortably on it in the sun. One girl is snuggled next to her,
talking; two others are tucking dolls into bed.

Again the drinking fountain gets used for washing animals. Some
children bring containers from the sand to fill with water; wet sand is
much more useful than dry sand. Later in the morning brooms, dust
pans, and a trash can are brought out by a teacher and used enthusiastically by children. There are lots of leaves to be swept.

This morning, with many things to do and with adult attentiveness to play, outdoor play goes on for an hour and no one asks if it's
time to go in. Everyone loses track of the time, in fact, until a
teacher notices in surprise that it's lunch time.

The staff had set up an environment outdoors that permitted all
kinds of play and language to flourish. The teacher permitted children
to help create the environment—to bring out things they thought they
would need and to go back in for more. Water play, spilling, combin-
ing and recombining materials, noise, moving one's body in many
different ways, even washing sandy animals in the drinking fountain
(which may have been against school rules but nobody wanted to
check) were permitted. Nobody got hurt, and "Teacher!" didn't get

yelled so often. By adding props, teachers transformed an environment that had not been working for children or adults into an environment that was interesting and pleasant for everyone.

Play needs plenty of props (although children who have mastered pretend play have less need for them than beginning players do [Smilansky & Shefatya, 1990, pp. 55, 72]). Without enough to do, children hurt themselves and each other, practice creative rule-breaking, and fuss or become lethargic. Adults find themselves policing rather than supporting play. With plenty of "loose parts" (Nicholson, 1974) that can be combined and recombined and that support the creation of complex play scripts, play goes on and on.

In this preschool even the observer, who knew about the theory of loose parts, was astonished at how much difference additional materials made. Teachers had thought it would be too much work to take things outside, but children were eager to help and were ready with requests for new items they thought might be interesting to take outside. Once children had enough to do, supervising their play became both easy and fun. Staff were no longer policing; instead, they had become property managers on a lively stage, and the play was a stellar production.

PROVIDING ENOUGH TIME

Stage managers are concerned with time as well as space and props. The more scene changes there are, the more entrances and exits, the harder the manager's task. Like plays in the theatre, programs for young children vary greatly in structure and pace. In a 3-hour, half-day program or a 10- to 12-hour child care day, the tempo may be relaxed or hurried, individualized or regimented. In some programs, the staff spends much time managing scene changes.

At Little Friends, a church-based child care program not far from Second Street School, three preschool classrooms share, on a rotating schedule, several common spaces: a small play yard, downstairs and outside; a large gym, upstairs (used in the evenings as a community recreation center); and a bathroom down the hall, which is also used by adults at work in the church offices and meeting rooms. Children are expected to move among these spaces in lines, ensuring reasonably orderly behavior in the halls. The day is tightly scheduled to make the space usable.

In keeping with the program's philosophy, group times are more valued than play times. The unhurried times of the day take place during meals and sharing circles, where adults sit with children and encourage conversation. Play times typically last for only half an hour, and clean-up follows each one. Children are free to play during less than a third of the day.

At Live Oak child care center, scheduling is quite different. There are four long blocks of time during the day when children are free to begin and end their own activities. The physical space facilitates this scheduling; bathrooms are in the classrooms, and there is direct access to the outdoors, making possible independent toileting and free indoor–outdoor movement. In addition, the scheduling reflects a conscious effort by staff to provide a relaxed pace and to interrupt children no more than necessary. For more than half the day, children are free to play.

Both morning and afternoon snacks are a choice, made available for half an hour or more until all interested children have eaten. As at Little Friends, group times serve to smooth transitions from one space to another, but once children are in a space they may choose freely for 1 to 2 hours. The long midday time when children don't choose— clean-up, lunch, and nap—has been planned so that morning and afternoon staff overlap to provide individualized attention to children and all the flexibility possible.

Live Oak, which has adopted the ideal of "day care as a good home" (Prescott, 1978), values the child's lived time more highly than the conveniences of institutional time. Little Friends, in contrast, could have been described by Suransky (1982) in *The Erosion of Childhood*.

> The concept of allowing a child to complete an activity he was engaged in was subordinate to the compelling nature of the *schedule*, which the teachers planned in advance of the children's experiences. The strict demarcation of the morning, by its very organization, denied the children the possibility of a continuous, uninterrupted activity brought to its natural closure. Instead, the structure was believed efficient by the staff (which indeed it was) and was intended to give the children a sense of security and consistency. While the children did appear to derive security from the temporal rigidity, they clearly became dependent on the structure and felt uncomfortable with any deviation. (p. 61)

Time, it is clear, can be managed in many ways. Some ways are responsive to young children's erratic pace and to the wide variation in pace among individuals, supporting autonomy and enabling children to exert initiative in largely uninterrupted play. Other ways are clock-controlled and group-focused, attempting to move all the children together. In such programs children get practice for the constraints they may later find in public school, but restricted opportunity to practice the initiative that is the developmental challenge for competent 3- to 5-year-olds.

Synchrony—precisely coordinated timing—is a basic characteristic of industrial society (Toffler, 1980). It is no historic accident that the clock has dominated the schoolroom wall and that every day in some kindergartens begins with "calendar." But as society moves from the rigidity of the assembly line to the flexibility made possible by computerization, our children may be better served by schooling that fosters their exploration and initiative, instead of schooling that fosters unquestioning obedience to clocks and calendars.

Obedience is a virtue in a stable society where the unexpected doesn't often happen. But in a rapidly changing society, children have greater need for confidence in the face of new problems to be solved. Children regularly encounter problems in their dealings both with the physical world and with other human beings, big and little. Teachers can help them to become increasingly independent problem solvers.

3 Teacher as Mediator

"Now, what do you do if you have any trouble with a friend?" asked the smiling teacher reviewing the kindergarten rules with the class.

"Tell the teacher," volunteered a boy.

"That's right," agreed the teacher. "Come straight to Mrs. Jordan, and she'll help you. Don't try to do it without my help. Teachers are here to help children be friends and work together nicely."

Predictably, "Teacher!" was often heard in this classroom, and the teacher could be counted on to solve children's problems for them. This approach teaches trust in helpful adults and dependence on them for resolving problems. In contrast, teachers of young children whose goal is the development of independent problem-solving skills sometimes adopt a laissez-faire approach: "Don't come to me. You figure it out." More effective, in modeling and explaining problem-solving skills that children can later practice on their own, is the teacher in the role of *mediator*.

TEACHING CONFLICT-RESOLUTION SKILLS

Young children at play frequently run afoul of each other in ways they can't handle on their own. Their agendas don't match, and they get in each other's way; sometimes the results are explosive. To protect them and, in the process, to teach them conflict-resolution skills they can use independently with each other, adult mediation is essential.

In Chapter 2, at Live Oak preschool we saw Dulcie encountering a bulldozer. "Mine!" she announced. But she wasn't the only worker in the sandbox. Bulldozing, she turned Marcos's figure—his carefully dug hole—into her ground, just part of the landscape to be flattened. Preschoolers do this a lot. Intent on their own play, they fail to notice that they've invaded someone else's territory. Marcos noticed; he socked Dulcie. Dulcie, surprised and indignant, socked him back.

John, a student teacher, saw them, and a series of possible reactions flashed through his mind. "Don't hit girls," his father would have said, but that's not what you say in preschool. When John was working in day care, Time Out would have been the next step, but for which child, he wondered—Marcos, Dulcie, or both? Here, no one uses Time Out; so what am I supposed to say? We don't hit. Use your words . . . and then what will they do?

While John was thinking, the teacher, who had also seen the incident, moved in.

"Marcos, what do you want to tell Dulcie?" she asks, squatting down between them. Marcos is crying; Dulcie socked him hard. Dulcie is annoyed; the teacher is in her bulldozer's way, a much more formidable obstacle than Marcos.

"I don't like her. She's a dumb-dumb," sobs Marcos.

"You're made at Dulcie. Can you tell her what she did to make you mad?"

"Hit me," says Marcos, sadly.

"You hit me first," says Dulcie, reasonably.

"Marcos, did you hit Dulcie?" the teacher asks. He nods. "Why?"

"My hole!" he wails, the memory of the violation of his play suddenly much more painful than the sore spot on his shoulder. "She messed my hole!" He tries to hit Dulcie again.

"What hole?" asks Dulcie, genuinely puzzled. "I didn't mess no hole."

"Can you show Dulcie your hole, Marcos?" the teacher asks. He certainly can.

"Here!" he shouts. "It was right here, and I digged it and digged it. . . ."

"Dulcie, Marcos is really sad about his hole," explains the teacher. "Do you think maybe you could help him fix it?"

Dulcie nods vigorously, grabbing her bulldozer.

"No!" says Marcos. "No 'dozer!"

"Do you want to fix the hole yourself, Marcos?" the teacher asks. He nods yes. "Then could you show Dulcie where to drive her bulldozer so she won't mess up your hole again?"

Marcos sketches a wide detour with his outstretched arm. Dulcie, following it, bulldozes off. Marcos wields his shovel, and his very important hole begins to take shape once more.

By focusing on the content of the play rather than on the violation of rules (We don't hit), the teacher has shown respect for both children's intent. She has used words to help them solve their very real problem and continue their play. The play is the important thing that's happening; problem-solving strategies should give priority to its continuation. In contrast, Time Out—stop playing and sit by yourself and think about what you've done—destroys the play and does not give young children useful strategies for solving either this problem or the next one that comes along.

In her role as mediator, the teacher asked genuine questions that enabled the children to use their words in effective communication to her and to each other. Among animals, children, and nations, territorial problems often lead to conflict. Here, Dulcie hadn't even noticed Marcos's territorial problem. They're only 3-year-olds, and he hasn't learned how to tell her. His teacher helped. By asking, "What do you want to tell Dulcie?" she suggested words as an alternative to both crying and hitting. Such suggestions, backed up by physical protection, build for the child a repertoire of his own strategies to draw on in times of need.

In territorial disputes, skilled teachers use clearly ordered words, as well as clearly ordered materials, to help children see figure–ground relationships: Dulcie, this is Marcos's hole. He really wants his hole right where he dug it. Can your road go way around his hole? He'll show you where.

Dulcie finds that reasonable, and way 'round she goes. Her bulldozer likes going way 'round. She didn't mean to mess Marcos's hole. She just didn't know it was there.

COMPLICATING PLAY TO KEEP IT SAFE

Having mediated this dispute, the teacher was free to move on to another activity. She decided to see what was happening indoors. She found the play dough table deserted, but as she sat down to talk to an observer, children began to join her. While rolling balls of dough, she suddenly wondered, "Why couldn't Rosie find a knife to slice her play dough? True, the tortilla press proved to be an inspiration, but where are those knives? And where are Matthew and Zach and Warren, last seen with the knives at the dough table? Are the heroes armed?"

The teacher goes to see. She finds boys and knives by the art supplies, where the boys have gone for string. Warren has wrapped the ball of string 'round and 'round his pants leg to hold a knife snugly against it, ready to hand in case of danger. Zach is struggling to cut

Warren's string from the ball so he, in turn, can have a sheath like Warren's.

"Need any help?" asks the teacher.

"Yeah," says Zach. "Cut it right here."

The teacher cuts it right there. "What are you making?" she asks.

"Brad, he's Shredder," explains Matthew eagerly. "He's the bad guy. The very bad guy. We scared him with our knives and he ran away. (No wonder Brad was smashing play dough, thinks the teacher.) We scared him. We scared him good. But he might come back. We're getting our knives ready for him. Can you cut this string, right here?"

"I'll bet he was really scared," says the teacher, "if you scared him with those real knives. I'd be scared too. I don't think he knew you were pretending. What did he do that was bad?"

"He dumped our doughnuts!" says Matthew indignantly. "We made 'em and we made 'em, and we were gonna eat 'em, and he yelled poo-poo and dumped 'em off the table and ran. So we took our knives and we scared him good! We scared him all over the yard. We let him get away, though. He ran real fast and we let him get away."

"Did anyone see you chasing Brad with knives?" asks the teacher, startled by this revelation. Where were the adults supervising the yard?

"Oh, we hid the knives," Matthew explains reassuringly. "Teachers don't like knives. We just showed them at Brad, and boy, was he scared!"

"Real scared!" confirms Zach.

"That's why we're stringing them on," says Warren. "They hide better that way."

Concealed weapons, thinks the teacher. Now that's all we need. "Why did Brad dump your doughnuts?" she asks.

"Shredder's bad!" they chorus. "Brad, he's Shredder and he's bad!"

"Does Shredder ever get hungry?" wonders the teacher. "Do you suppose Brad was hungry and wanted a doughnut, and you had all the doughnuts, and he was trying to get one?"

"No, Shredder's just bad," Matthew insists.

"I'm hungry," says Zach. "We need some more doughnuts. Let's go, Turtles!"

"Can Brad have some doughnuts too?" the teacher asks.

"He can be Leonardo," Matthew decides. "He's not Shredder any more. Hey, Brad, you're Leonardo! Want a doughnut? We're making doughnuts."

This scenario reflects the ideas of both Carlsson-Paige and Levin (1987) and Paley (1984, 1988) about teacher intervention in weapons play. Had the teacher seen Brad actually threatened with knives, even blunt kitchen knives, she would have intervened at once to keep everyone safe. Instead, she missed that part of the action and was inadvertently available at the play dough table to help a rejected Brad express his anger and find a new focus for play.

Weapons are unavailable as play props in this classroom, and the children knew teachers don't like knives, so they concealed them. This action had clear defensive intent, and no one was endangered, and the boys were busy elaborating it when the teacher intervened. As mediator she found out more about the script, showed them that she respected it, and helped them expand on it. Her suggestion that Shredder might have been hungry was first rejected by Matthew—"No, Shredder's just bad"—but it made a connection with Zach, who was ready for more doughnuts. Outfoxed by a good idea, Matthew capitulated gracefully and invited Brad back into the play he had rejected earlier. And the knives went back to the play dough table, where they belonged. The teacher stayed alert so they didn't get taken off again.

Paley (1988) comments at the end of an extraordinary account of mediation between invisible Mr. Nobodys rejecting their responsibility for clean-up after "doll corner smashie," they "love it when I behave sensibly" (p. 102). Sensibly, that is, within the rules of the children's script. Matthew's teacher was able to resist the temptation to impose adults' "sensible" rules—no chasing, no threatening, the knives stay at the table. Through her forebearance, the play and its complex meanings were sustained, and she was able to extend the children's understanding through genuine questioning (Paley, 1986b) rather than shame them through moralizing. Teacher as mediator is not simply managing behavior; she is teaching social skills and suggesting ideas to enrich play. Her goals include the development of both empathy and divergent thinking.

PROBLEM SOLVING TO SUSTAIN PLAY

The teacher mediates between children and also between a child and the sometimes recalcitrant physical world. String and dull scissors may simply be too much for a preschooler and require direct assistance. But a child tugging at a wagon whose wheel is wedged behind a board can be helped to notice the source of the problem and thus to solve it for herself. David Hawkins (1974) has described this kind of help as "completing the circuit" for children. He proposes an electronic analogy.

> Think of circuits that have to be completed. Things go out along one bundle of channels, something happens, and signals come back along another bundle of channels; and there's some sort of feedback involved. Children are not always able to sort all of this feedback for themselves. The adult's function, in all the child's learning, is to provide a kind of external loop, to provide a selective feedback from the child's own choice and action. The child's involvement gets some response from an adult and this in turn is made available to the child. The child is learning about himself through his joint effects on the non-human *and* the human world around him.
>
> The function of the teacher, then, is to respond diagnostically and helpfully to a child's behavior, to make what he considers to be an appropriate response, a response which the child needs to complete the process he's engaged in at a given moment. (p. 53)

There are frequent periods, Hawkins makes clear, when children don't need the external loop. But

> When they do need it and there's no one around to contribute the adult resonance, then they're not always able to carry on the process of investigation, of inquiry and exploration, of learning, because they need help over a hump that they can't surmount through their own resources. If help isn't available, the inquiry will taper off, and that particular episode, at least, will have failed to accomplish what it otherwise might have. (p. 54)

What kinds of "humps" do children encounter as they play? How can adults help?

> At Second Street child care center the outdoor environment for the 3-year-olds is well provisioned with a climber, bikes, sand area with tools, a playhouse, and a number of milk crates. The children have dispersed to the various activities. A girl and two boys have started a chase game. Several children have attached themselves to their teacher. They hold her hands as she walks around the yard, a reassuring presence, talking with children in a friendly way, helping to sort out traffic jams on the bike path. For a short while she pulls a

wagon with two children in it. "Victor, are you all right?" she calls, moving in his direction as he yells from across the yard. Her message is consistent: I'm paying attention; you can tell me how you're feeling.

Now she is helping Marina, Ebony, and Annie organize crates into a roadside stand, at which they sit to sell things—tickets to the beach and to Disneyland, and ice cream, as the play develops—to the passersby. As the teacher moves on, the aide arrives. They sell him a ticket and give him change. He helps them rebuild the crates, two of which have fallen.

MARINA: Knock, knock.

AIDE (*moving another crate*): Oh, knock knock on the door? Now you've got doors. (*Marina gives him directions, then tells him something else.*) Can I have change? Got something else to drink? You can stop Ruben when he comes by and give him a ticket. Ruben, you can stop there and get your ticket.

THE GIRLS (*to Ruben, on his bike*): Ruben. (*He comes for a ticket, and they turn to Ricky*) Ricky, want a ticket? (*He speeds by without stopping.*)

AIDE: Okay, is the door back there? How are you?

MARINA: Fine.

Traffic on the path increases. A heavy load goes by—a boy on a bike with a trailer, with a girl in the trailer pulling two more boys in a wagon! Hearing a squabble at a roadside stand, the aide responds, "Don't tease her. You sell your tickets, and she can sell hers." A boy joins the ticket sellers. There's an argument over territory. The aide tells one of the girls, "Tell 'em you had it first."

Unskilled players, a category that includes many 3-year-olds, are helped to sustain the focus of their play by adult ideas, physical assistance—the crates are big and bulky—and intervention in disputes. This aide, who used to moralize a lot (see Chapter 5), is learning to enter into play and to keep it foremost as he helps with problem solving. By modeling appropriate behavior, he helps children keep the play going. When he falls back into less skilled interventions, the teacher models for the children and for himself, too.

The block area is supplied with a dozen large pieces of heavy cardboard—dismantled packing boxes—a wonderful resource for creating little houses of one's own. In a small space with 3-year-olds, some of whom attack instead of using words, territory is a frequent issue. There are many opportunities for problem solving.

> AIDE (*responding to a dispute*): Victor, what are you doing to Andy? Don't do that. (*Andy, unsatisfied, goes over to the teacher.*)
>
> TEACHER (*hugging Andy*): Andy doesn't like that, Victor. He's very upset. It hurts him when you do that. (*To Andy*) Go get a drink.
>
> RUBEN (*in dressups, succeeding after a struggle to get a dress on*): Teacher, lookit.
>
> TEACHER: Oh boy, are you dressed to kill. Look at that RED dress. (*Hearing a wail from the cardboard houses*) Tell Jerry you need your blanket back. Annie needs her blanket back, Jerry. (*To Andy, who has put on a flowered skirt*) You got a new outfit.
>
> The teacher soothes Annie, who has followed her. She helps Annie fix a new space for herself and gets her a stuffed rabbit and a blanket. When Marina comes over to play, the teacher demonstrates for her: "Here's the door. Knock. Knock knock. Can I come in?"

On this morning both adults were able to be playful. They were giving information to the children about materials and ideas for their play and about getting along with each other, but they were doing so as co-players rather than in a teacher-like fashion. When adults intervene within the script, children are helped to sustain it.

These were young 3-year-olds at the beginning of the day care year. They were exploring the physical environment, first and foremost, with some successful forays into sustained dramatic play. Here they needed, and got, lots of help from the adults, who were working hard. Continual involvement seems to be unavoidable at the beginning of the year, when it's up to adults to help children learn how to play with the materials and with each other—to socialize them into the culture of day care. And to reassure them that this is a safe place to be, with caring adults.

4 Teacher as Player

When should an adult participate in children's play? The adults in the 3-year-old class described in Chapter 3 moved in and out of play to model and mediate. They acted as builder's helper, customer at the roadside stand, admirer of new fashion, and visitor knocking at the door. In all these roles, they helped to sustain the play while responding to children's ideas.

"CALL MIKEY"

At Live Oak child care center, another teacher imaginatively role-played solutions to a pretend homemaker's real problem.

As the teacher approaches the housekeeping area, Paula tells him the oven door won't close.

TEACHER: Call someone to come and fix it.

PAULA (*phone in hand*): What's the number?

TEACHER (*one number at a time as Paula dials*): 282–4761.

PAULA (*into phone*): Can you come and fix our stove? He says yes.

TEACHER: How much does he charge?

PAULA: What do you charge? (*calling to the teacher*) $1,500.

TEACHER: $1,500! Oh no, tell him no. Call Mikey.

PAULA: What number?

TEACHER: 792–3594.

PAULA (*into phone*): Mikey, can you come fix our stove? (*calling to teacher*) He says yes!

TEACHER: Is he coming? What does he charge?

PAULA: $3.00.

TEACHER: That's better. (*Alan comes into the housekeeping area.*) Are you Mikey?

ALAN: Yes!

Deciding whether or not to participate in children's play requires thought about children's need for challenge, their skills in sustaining play, and one's own preferred teaching style. Some skilled teachers feel that an adult's place is outside the play. Some look for opportunities to add materials or ideas. Some join in frequently; they like to play, and they feel their participation builds relationships with children and enriches the content of the play.

"DON'T LET THE BABIES DIE"

The preschool in the following episode has a prop box of medical supplies in frequent use. Several weeks earlier the teacher was an active participant in hospital play, helping Sarah use CPR to resuscitate her doll, Bubbles. Today the dolls are sick again.

Sarah begins by explaining, "Bubbles is sick, and her brother, Peapod. This is the only girl who is not sick. Her name is Heather." Lia and Liana go to the house area and bring many blankets, while Sarah builds with hollow blocks. She gets the plastic ironing board, which had previously served as an operating table for Bubbles.

LIA: We got a pillow for her.

SARAH: I need to put her in my safe house.

LIANA: Lots of people work on a baby that has this. They check her heart. Use the stick.

SARAH: She has CPR. Her heart is beating too fast. She might throw up.

JOSEPH (*very seriously*): I don't think your baby is going to be all right. She's going to have to go to heaven.

SARAH (*smiling*): I know!

JOSEPH: I saw a huge cut on her.

SARAH: I think both our babies are going to die.

TEACHER: That would be so sad.

TRAVIS: Don't let the babies die.

LIANA: We shouldn't let Sarah's die. That would make her so sad.

TEACHER: What about the other one?

LIANA: We should try not to let that one die either. I'm working on some stuff. (*She wraps a syringe and some medical supplies in a piece of paper.*)

SARAH: She has a bigger cut than we thought.

LIANA: I'm wrapping a message up from on the surgery.

TEACHER: When is surgery?
SARAH: Surgery is after snack.
TEACHER: Will she be okay?
SARAH: Yes!

(Linda Torgerson, teacher/observer)

In her earlier participation as a surgeon, the teacher had introduced CPR. Today she observes without comment that CPR has become a symptom, not a treatment. She does, however, comment when Sarah seems pleased that the babies are going to die. "That would be so sad," she says, and the children pick up on her concern and devote their energies to healing. Because the children are accustomed to her involvement as a co-player, they experience her concern about the babies as that of a medical colleague or family member, rather than as an intrusive adult telling them how they're supposed to feel.

SHOPPING AT FEDCO

The teacher at Second Street preschool loves to play with children. She has learned not to do it too much, but sometimes she joins in, as stage director and player, to encourage children to elaborate their spontaneous dramatic play. This episode begins with a discussion at group time.

TEACHER: Yesterday Yolanda and Luz were playing Shopping at Fedco. I wondered if more people would like to play Shopping at Fedco today? It's a big store. There's room for lots of people. What do you need to go shopping? Let's make a list. (*She has taped a big sheet of paper to the wall and writes children's suggestions on it.*)
YOLANDA: I take my purse.
LUZ: Me too.
TEACHER: You dressed up yesterday. I saw you in a purple dress.
YOLANDA: And high heels.
TEACHER: And high heels. Do men shop at Fedco too?
LUZ: No. Only mamas.
BEN: My dad goes to the store. My mom stays home.
TEACHER: Do men work at the store?
MOHAMMED: They put things in bags.
TEACHER: So we need bags in our store. What else do we need?

SARAH: Bread.

LUZ: Oranges. And milk.

TEACHER: I'm going to write groceries. We call food at the store groceries.

BEN: Shopping basket.

YOLANDA: My mama buyed some dishes.

TEACHER: What did she pay for them with?

YOLANDA: The lady gave her some money.

TEACHER: People take money to the store. Sometimes they get money back too. Today I'm going to be the store manager so lots of people can play. The store will open in 5 minutes. If you want to go shopping, get dressed up. Put some money in your purse. If you want to work in the store, come help me fix it up.

Five minutes later, the teacher leads the class in a countdown: "Five, four, three, two, one . . . Store's open."

Yolanda, in high heels, purple dress, and shoulder bag, has been waiting in line, admiring the silver paper squares she has found for money. She picks up a shopping basket and goes first to a shelf where she puts dishes in her basket. Then she strolls to a table where there is a pile of plastic food. She adds some to her basket. Luz hands her an egg, which she carefully tucks in. She spends several moments trying to find a place to balance a slice of bread.

Hiking up her shoulder bag, she continues to the checkout counter, where the teacher has positioned Mohammed with a supply of large paper bags. He dumps Yolanda's basket on the floor and transfers its contents, one by one, to the bag. She waits graciously.

Ben, at the cash register, is prompted by the store manager/ teacher and asks, "Where's your money?" Yolanda pulls out a handful of silver, giving it to Ben. He rings it up on the cash register and gives it back.

Yolanda says "thank you" sweetly and heads home with her bag full.

What did the children gain from the teacher's direction of their play? Their going-shopping script was expanded to include list-making, money, shopping bags, and male players, none of which had been included in the original play. These were the teacher's ideas, introduced because she thinks they're good ideas. In this morning's play, she has taken the initiative away from the children.

It worked, nevertheless, because this teacher is genuinely playful. She has a good sense of the children's interests and capacities and a comfortable relationship with them; they're not intimidated by her and enjoy her participation. She helps them feel important. Her involvement relieved them, for a day, of the need to spend energy on inventing a script, negotiating conflicts, and solving interpersonal problems. If she structured it this way every day, they'd miss out on a lot of important learning. She doesn't; the next day, the store play was theirs again. Several weeks later the shopping script was still being enacted at the children's initiation.

PICNIC

With a group of 3-year-olds inclined toward "herd behavior," as he describes it, this teacher at Live Oak child care center has decided to take the lead with a new dramatic play idea and encourage the children to join him. It's his hope that the next time they'll do it themselves, freeing him to move on to the blocks or puzzles and encourage more involvement there. His presence, he has found, attracts children to wherever he is, and he uses it thoughtfully.

It's a brisk but sunny day. During snack, the children are engaged in leisurely conversation. The teacher also uses this time to suggest choices that will be available at play time: "I'm going to be in the play house area. And I'll open the back door. We haven't had a picnic for a long time. Some of the babies might like to go on a picnic—but it's pretty cold today so they'll need clothes."

For awhile, nearly all the children are more interested in the new play dough than in a picnic. But eventually Derek remembers. He asks the teacher, and they talk about what they will need.

TEACHER: Would you like to take the blue blanket? (*He gets it.*)
Now, what else are we going to need to take outside?
DEREK: Cups.
TEACHER: Cups, and . . .
DEREK: We have some cookies. We need to make them.
TEACHER: Do you remember where the cups are? (*He does. Anthony runs to join them.*) Would you like to join us on our picnic, Anthony? (*Anthony nods happily.*) What else do we need?
DEREK: A drink. Hot dogs. I gonna make some hot dogs.
TEACHER: Anthony, want to bring out some of the babies? (*He does.*)
DEREK: I can't find the hot dogs.
Julie has taken a broom outside; she's sweeping around the blanket, which is on the little porch outside the door.

TEACHER: Hi, Carlos. Would you like to bring your baby on the picnic too? Do the babies need clothes?

ANTHONY and CARLOS: No. No clothes.

CARLOS: I laid my baby down.

ANTHONY: My baby's gonna sleep.

CARLOS: I gonna take my baby to the bathroom. (*He does. Derek has gone outside, leaving the pot of "hot dogs" on the stove.*)

TEACHER: It's not burning, is it? Should I go check it? (*Derek goes to check the pot on the stove.*)

DEREK (*stirring the pot*): Zoom, zoom, zoom. It's ready! It's ready! You guys share. I got some straws.

ANTHONY: I'll give me some drink of water. (*Children, babies, and teacher settle down on the blanket for a picnic.*)

JULIE: The baby's crying, guys.

CARLOS: I know.

Response to the teacher's picnic idea was delayed, as children's response often is. Adults can afford to toss ideas out and wait to see what happens; they have lots more. Children will respond, now or later, to those ideas that make connections for them.

Picnic, a play script familiar to Derek, interested him and got him the teacher to play with. Anthony, Carlos, and Julie may have been attracted not by the prospect of a picnic but by the teacher's, or Derek's, presence in the playhouse. There are many good starting points for play.

"CAN X-RAY SEE THIS LADY?"

Other teachers have taken a planfully active role in play with children whose family culture is different from that of the school, teaching them the play scripts of the culture represented by the school in order to help them in the task of becoming bilingual or bicultural. This teacher, working with school-age Aboriginal children in central Australia, involves herself in sociodramatic play as a language and role model.

The play area is set up as a medical clinic. The teacher is playing nurse; children are playing doctor, patient, and X-ray technician.

NURSE (*teacher*): Will you attend to this patient, please?

DOCTOR: What's the trouble?

PATIENT: I've got a broken arm.

DOCTOR (*holding phone*): Ring, ring.
X-RAY: Hello.
DOCTOR: Ah—what do I say?
NURSE: Just ask if X-ray can see this lady.
DOCTOR: Is X-ray ready to see another lady?
X-RAY: What?
DOCTOR: Can X-ray have another lady there for X-ray?

The children and teacher . . . had just visited the Central Australian Aboriginal Congress health centre and observed and talked with a doctor, nurse, and receptionist there. As the children began this role playing they knew quite a lot about medical settings, but they needed some help with words and phrases to link with the actions they had observed and discussed. (Sparrow, 1988, pp. 233–234, 236)

Children from a culture with its own traditional healing practices have a longer bridge to cross into the mysteries of Western medicine than the children who were scheduling surgery for Bubbles and Peapod. Through play children begin to understand the mysteries of the culture into which they are growing.

The teacher playing nurse was trained in elementary education, where teachers typically do not play with children. But in the public school in which she is working, play "is not a peripheral sideline to the serious job of adults and children at school. It does not simply provide a spontaneous interlude to the more structured work of the classroom" (Sparrow, 1988, p. 234). Rather, play is basic to the kindergarten/primary language program.

By involving herself at a variety of levels in this play the teacher helps children understand the role requirements of the interaction, in terms of both action and language. . . . Over the three to four weeks of the theme, as the play becomes more complicated, the teacher needs only to provide some specific suggestions; and near the end of the theme she does not intervene at all. (Sparrow, 1988, p. 236)

WHY TEACHERS PLAY

Some teachers enter play spontaneously, for their own pleasure or the children's. They take their cues from the children, and the relationship is one of mutuality. Other teachers make conscious use of play for teaching purposes. Inherent in the role of *teacher as player* is the risk that the adult will take over, directing play that then ceases to be the children's, or will attract children looking for adult attention.

When is this risk most appropriately taken? We believe it is at beginnings, when children are still short on ideas for play in the school setting and/or skills for playing with materials and each other. There are several kinds of beginnings, including beginning child care as a young 3-year-old or entering a school culture different from one's home culture.

The Picnic sequence, like the play events with crates and cardboards described at the end of Chapter 3, involved adults in play with young 3-year-olds early in the year. Their goal was to *get play started*, to give children ideas and skills to be added to their repertoires. As the children became more competent players, adults were free to play and mediate less and to observe and assess in more depth.

Teachers of children who come to school unfamiliar with its materials, language, or play scripts may need to enter into play with children to build bridges from home culture to school culture. Children become competent with materials not through directed practice but through exploratory play. They become competent with oral language through spontaneous exploration of its sounds and its potential for communication. They become competent with scripts of their home and neighborhood by playing them. For the young child, competence at school is learned through play. The "concentrated language encounter" of "Can X-Ray See This Lady?" is a teacher–child interaction designed to orient Aboriginal children to Australian school language by re-creating the informal sort of conversation that mothers have with their children (Sparrow, 1988). Similarly, working with immigrant children in Israel, Smilansky (1968) has entered play in order to teach them the dramatic play scripts appropriate to the Israeli preschool.

Bridges are built from both ends. It is important that teachers also take initiative in becoming more familiar with the materials, language, and events of children's home cultures and introduce them into activities at school—not just on special occasions but as part of the daily play environment. All children should have access to both familiar and new cultural modes; thus it is important to implement an antibias curriculum (Derman-Sparks & A.B.C. Task Force, 1989) for the middle-class white children whose experience traditional schooling has matched most closely. In doing so, teachers as well as children will find themselves challenged to learn new play scripts.

Some teachers prefer to provision the environment for changing dramatic play themes while making a conscious decision to stay out of the play themselves. "If I'm playing grocery store, children will come because I'm there," said one kindergarten teacher. "I want them to come because the play itself has meaning for them." In contrast, the teacher playing Picnic is willing to use his presence as the initial attraction for his 3-year-olds, trusting that the play will take over.

5 Teacher Behavior That Interrupts Play

It is inevitable that some play will be interrupted by adults. Some interruptions are accidental; the adult wasn't playing close attention to the script. Others are intentional; the adult has a different agenda and believes it is more important than the play. Both teacher as mediator and teacher as player risk interrupting children's play—taking it over, or destroying it altogether for the sake of teaching something they value more. If teachers care about sustaining play, they must tailor their interventions to conform to the script the children are playing.

Children's dramatic play is a form of improvisational theatre that draws its scripts from their imaginary and real life experiences. In improvising, children often interrupt each other's scripts, which is one reason teachers are called upon as mediators. Sometimes these interruptions take place within cooperative dramatic play, when the players discover that their versions of the script differ from each other. At these points they may move out of role temporarily to argue the point; for example, "We don't need two bus drivers; no bus has two drivers!" (Smilansky & Shefatya, 1990, p. 23). Children, however, negotiate as peers; whereas if an all-knowing adult moves to set the play straight with her version of the script, she can easily take away the initiative from the children.

INTERRUPTING FOR ONE'S OWN PLEASURE IN PLAY

Adults relatively new to teaching, or reassessing their teaching, may try different approaches at different times to see what will happen. Here, for example, are two different sequences of "kitty" play by the same children on different days. During the first, the teacher simply watched, taking notes.

Julie and Katie are in the book area, meowing. Derek comes in and says, "Here's some milk" as he puts down a green plastic saucepan.

Katie and Julie crawl to the pan and put their heads down, but Julie pushes just a little and has the pan to herself. Derek goes back to the cupboard, gets two more pans, and calls them over: "Here kitty kitty kitty, here kitty kitty." Katie and Julie crawl toward the new pans.

DEREK (*to David*): These are not babies. These are kittens.

ANTHONY: They need to go to the vet's. They need to go to the vet's.

DEREK: Come on, kitties. . . . I took them.

ANTHONY: They're going to the vet's. (*The children all move to the pillows in the book area.*)

DEREK: That's not cat food. Cat food has water. They have to have water. I need my fork. Open your mouth, kitty. . . . The cat has an owie. I'll take him to the vet.

ANTHONY: I'm making good food for them. They don't like that stuff. This is cake. Know what this is? Cake for them.

NICOLE: Here kitty. (*Scooping with spoon in pan*) Open your mouth, kitty. Now are you hungry?

ANTHONY: I need a pot. That's more. That's the same thing.

What do kitties do, and what do people do with kitties? Children who share common experiences can play Kitty, or any other script, together. These children know, collectively, that kitties drink milk and eat cat food from dishes on the floor, that they don't walk on their hind legs, and that they come when you call kitty kitty kitty. Sometimes they need to go to the vet, especially if they have an owie. Feeding is a daily event in the life of cats and their people; going to the vet is a dramatic, occasional event. Children weave both the daily and the dramatic into their play; they need to understand both.

Even though Derek reminded David, "These are not babies. These are kittens," the temptation to give animals human characteristics can't be resisted altogether. "Open your mouth, kitty," say two different children, feeding kitties with a fork and spoon. And cat food—"they don't like that stuff"—is rejected in favor of cake.

There are, nonetheless, clear rules to the play. On another day, when the teacher spontaneously joined in, the play was changed dramatically.

JULIE: Meow, meow.

DEREK: Woof, woof.

NICOLE: Meow, meow, meow.

LARUE (*putting on the white lab coat and the plastic safari hat*): There's my suit.

KATIE and NICOLE (*pawing at the knees of the teacher*): Meow, meow, meow. (*At this point the teacher gets down on her knees, puts her hands up as paws, and begins meowing.*)

JULIE: You can't be a cat!

TEACHER (*forlornly*): Meow.

JULIE: You're a teacher! You have to sit in that chair! (*She points to it.*)

TEACHER: But I know how to meow like a kitty.

DEREK (*pointing at David, who is lying on the floor with his eyes closed*): Uh oh! The kitty died. (*The group stops and looks. No one moves or says anything.*)

TEACHER: What can we do? It's an emergency.

DEREK: I don't know.

TEACHER: We could go to the phone. Who should we call? (*There is no response. The children look at the teacher.*) Okay, I'll go dial 911. (*She does.*) Hello? Yes? We have an emergency at Live Oak Child Care Center at 1145 High Street. In the Sunshine Room. We have a kitty who appears to be dead!

DEREK (*putting the fire hat on his head and holding his hand with the thumb toward his ear*): Okay—I'm on my way. OOO - OOO - OOO. (*Children begin lying on the floor, eyes closed.*)

TEACHER: How can we help the kitties? (*Larue gets a bowl and spoon and begins to feed them medicine.*)

DAVID (*jumping up*): I'm alive! I'm alive!

Others do the same. David falls back down. Another child tries to take the bowl and spoon from Larue, who says, "No, I'm the nurse!" There are now nine children in the house, block and book areas, dying and reviving. Anthony comes in and out to help.

In these children's definition of proper roles, grown-ups don't play kitty. When the adult moved into the kitty role, the play was interrupted. She had left the role the children had defined for her by meowing and pawing at her—Person Who Takes Care of Kitties—to become a kitty herself. Why? As an experiment, perhaps, to see what the children would do, or as a spontaneous bit of play on her part, because she was feeling playful. But the children were having none of it. Children play, they remind her. Teachers sit in chairs and take care of children—and kitties.

It took Derek's and David's invention of Dead Kitty to get the

play back on track, with the teacher moving into a clearly grown-up
role: helper in an emergency. "What can we do?" she asks. They don't
know. She takes over, introducing a call-911 script, until Derek is able
to plug into it by becoming a firefighter responding to the call. Once
that happens, many children are able to collaborate in a dying, helping, and reviving script, without further teacher intervention.

The children's temporary immobilization may have been a response to the shock of Dead Kitty. But this was, as it turned out, a
familiar dramatic script that they all knew how to play. More shock-
ing, perhaps, was their teacher's transformation into kitty; that wasn't
in their script. The appropriate role for an adult in children's play is
defined by children; they expect an adult to play their game, not her
own.

These 3-year-olds were looking for a person who takes care of
kitties. They were also reality-based in their distinction between children and adults and their respective places in the world: Adults are
people who take care of children.

We asked another teacher at Live Oak, who spends much of her
time with the 4-year-olds, "How do you play with the children?"

"Well," she said, "I taste things when they pretend to feed them to
me. If they chortle, 'That's poison!' and laugh maniacally because
they've tricked me—'Ha ha, you trusted us!'—I fall down dead. If they
meow at me, I purr. Sometimes I initiate growling, because they like to
run away scared. If they scare me, I'm properly frightened."

This is a playful young adult, but she has made a clear definition
of appropriate play behaviors with children. She is willing to play
victim of poisoning if older 4-year-olds, who know they're pretending,
assign her that role in their play, but it isn't a role she would ever invent
if they offered her pretend food. She is the gracious recipient of gifts
that aren't poisoned. If they mew at her as kittens, she purrs as a
mother cat. She can sometimes growl at them, as an adult bear might
growl at cubs, because they have previously initiated games of scaring
her and know how such games are played; as she says, "They like to
run away scared."

These are all adult roles, spilling over into the sorts of games that
parents play with their children and that are safe because the relationship is safe. Hiding and finding, growling and running, poisoning and
reviving are all games of separation and reunion—important themes in
the lives of young children. If you leave me at day care, do you love
me? Will I be cared for? Will you come back?

This adult does not play at being a child. "If they asked me to be a
baby (which they don't), I'd say 'I don't feel like it.' It wouldn't work.

The kids would get self-conscious, and the play would center around me." Children's babies, in play, can be dolls and each other, but not adults.

When things are going smoothly, the natural relationship between caring adult and children is power *for*. Power exercised *for* a child means that the child is provided experiences that contribute to the development of self-esteem and confidence and thus create power for the child. From the child's point of view, the child is facilitated (Trook, 1983). The relationship is asymmetrical; the adult cares for the child and consciously nurtures his growth.

Sometimes, the power relationship can change to a more balanced form of power sharing, power *with*. When power is used *for* the child, the adult is intentionally guiding, structuring, or supporting toward a goal. When power *with* occurs, adult and child share a sense of wonder and are creating together (Trook, 1983). Following the child's lead in play, the adult has no agenda other than mutual interaction with the child.

The teacher playing kitty had no agenda other than mutual interaction, but she failed to follow the children's lead. Play scripts are in the children's charge; the adult player may not move beyond the script as the children define it.

Here's an example of two adults playing within the script to create power *with*.

At Madison West preschool, where today the kitchen area has been set up outdoors, Sharon and Tamara are at the stove. Laurie is by the hanging clothes, adorned in red high heels, a purple dress, and a turquoise shawl, holding a baby doll in each arm. Jorge, clad in a firefighter's suit, wheels a wooden stroller. "Look, Tamara!" he says.

Three small plastic dishes, red, yellow, and green, sit on the concrete, filled with mixtures of sand and water. Tamara scoops some from one dish to another. Laurie pours water from a teakettle into one dish, but Tamara says, "No! Don't do that!" She looks at me and asks, "You hungry?"

I nod yes. Tamara carries over a cup, lifts the green dish, and sets them on the table I sit against. She goes back to the stove, where she sets a pot in the oven and closes the oven door. She opens it to put a lid on the pot, closes it, opens it again and pushes in another pot.

During this time, Sharon has been washing dishes with invisible water. Now she turns to Tamara and asks, "They all clean now?" Tamara nods approval and walks to me.

TAMARA (*with a look of concern on her face*): You tell me you
  want some spinach?
ME: I'd love some spinach.
TAMARA: Good! 'Cause that what I made. (*She dishes some of her
  mind's spinach onto my plate.*)
LAURIE (*to Tamara, who is on her way back to the kitchen*): Did
  you put on clothes today?
TAMARA: No.
LAURIE: These are my high heels. (*She lifts one dainty foot.*)
TAMARA (*walking with Laurie to the rack where dresses are hang-
  ing*): Let me see. What kinds of dresses? Let me see, if I wear
  . . . should I wear *this* dress to the party? You want to wear this
  one? (*She holds out a different dress for each of them.*)
LAURIE: Oh, yes. (*She drapes the new dress around her shoulder,
  as a scarf for the one she's already wearing.*)
TAMARA (*with a pan in her hand, walking to the
  teacher*): Teacher, I brought you something.
TEACHER: What is it?
TAMARA: Spinach.
TEACHER: Spinach—mmm—would you bring me some broccoli?
  You know I love broccoli and mushrooms. (*Tamara runs back
  to the stove and fills four dishes with sand and water.*)
TAMARA (*handing the dish to the teacher*): Here's your broccoli.
TEACHER: This is broccoli? And these are mushrooms?
TAMARA: Uh-hum. (*She runs to me.*) Here's mushrooms.
ME: Umm, thank you, delicious.

                                                        (Solow, 1989)

This is play as genuine dialogue among children and between
Tamara and the two adults. Both adults respond playfully and spon-
taneously; the teacher introduces broccoli not as new vocabulary for
Tamara but because she really doesn't want spinach.

Those rare, mutually creative interactions which are the high point of our
human existence are possible only with peers. Thus it is clear that our
liberation is directly related to our ability to be liberators, i.e., to help
others, including children, create the power that makes them our peers as
often as possible. (Trook, 1983, p. 16)

Trook's use of the word *liberation* reflects Freire's (1970) assertion
that all education either domesticates or liberates. Power *with* equal-
izes, temporarily, the imbalance between the adult and child, making

them peers in play. They both contribute good ideas, but the child retains the lead—because play is, after all, the child's world. In the play just described, the interactions are characterized by mutuality, and the child is, for the moment, no less competent than the adult.

In this episode, Tamara invited the adults to participate in her smoothly running play. When things aren't going so smoothly, responsible adults may need to intervene without being invited. Skilled mediators respond in a power *for* mode, taking the children's script seriously as they suggest alternatives for problem solving. In contrast, adults who don't mind interrupting children's play use their power *on* children, arbitrarily replacing children's agendas with their own. Power *on* is used to domesticate, to help children learn how to behave.

INTERRUPTING TO TEACH RULES

Andy and Ruben are carefully building a platform of blocks for their cars, with an elegant double ramp leading off the platform. Ricky's fast car crashes into the ramp. Andy hits Ricky.

RICKY (*running to the aide*): Andy hit me! (*Ebony and Marina start pushing their cars down the ramp.*)

ANDY (*wailing*): No, no, no!

AIDE: Andy, come over here. You can't play if you can't share. Use your words. Don't just say No, no, no. Tell him to stop. (*Andy is silent. He tries to twist away and get back to his blocks. The aide restrains him.*) When I call you, I expect an answer. (*Andy runs back to the blocks.*)

RUBEN: Look what I'm making, guys. (*He starts to run his car on the ramp. Andy pushes Ruben's car away, and the ramp falls down.*)

AIDE: Andy, remember what we talked about. (*Andy runs to the teacher for help.*)

TEACHER (*calling across the room*): Ruben, I want you and Andy to help put that bridge back together.

Ruben quietly complies. Then Andy starts building a tower; Ruben hands blocks to him. When the tower falls, it falls on Ricky, who laughs loudly. Andy laughs too. Ruben starts running a car down the ramp. Andy is rebuilding his tower, with Ricky helping him this time. When it falls, Andy laughs loudly. Ricky echoes him.

ANDY (*exulting*): It fell down!

RICKY (*also delighted*): It fell down!

ANDY: Two, two . . .

AIDE: Andy, do you understand? Not so loud. Use your inside
voices.

Andy hit Ricky because Ricky carelessly messed up his careful
construction. But Andy became the culprit because Ricky complained
to the aide. The aide's response was power *on* moralizing: "Andy,
come over here. You can't play if you can't share." Andy's agenda—to
protect his blocks—was ignored.

Escaping back to his play. Andy took out his frustration on his
friend Ruben. The aide admonished Andy again, and Andy turned to
the teacher—who asked Ruben to be a helpful friend. That turned out
to be a power *for* intervention, because Ruben was more than willing
to help. The play resumed, and Ricky got into it too. But if Andy were
a less determined block builder, the aide's interruptions to teach rules
could have effectively destroyed his play, perhaps leaving Andy sulk-
ing or lashing out rather than constructively engaged in play. The aide
consistently ignored children's play agendas, intervening only on be-
half of adult standards: "You have to share." "Use your words." "Not so
loud."

Power *on* fails to teach children problem-solving strategies they
can use independently. Instead, it encourages immediate appeal to
authority: "Teacher, he hit me." Since the adult may not have seen the
sequence of events, his solutions are likely to be arbitrary, falling back
on rules of behavior while ignoring the content of the play. "I don't
care what's happening to your ramp, you have to learn to share. And
when I call you, I expect an answer." Children in power *on* classrooms
tattle a lot, hoping to get authority on their side first. They don't try to
work things out with each other.

Power *on* is appropriate and necessary when safety is involved. It
may be appropriate if the adult has a moral lesson to teach and
believes it can be taught directly. But power *on* ignores and interrupts
play.

Effective facilitation—power *for*—takes the script and rhythm of
the play into account, even when there are conflicts to be solved.

Back at Live Oak preschool, Brad and Danny, with Matthew and Michael on the periphery, are playing a fantasy script in the roles of
Mr. T and Hannibal. Their props include hollow blocks, unit blocks,
trucks, small traffic signs, cars and planes, and Lincoln logs. The dialogue is loud and fast-paced.
BRAD: Who said you could play? Nobody said you could play.
DANNY: I'm Hannibal.

BRAD: No, I'm first.

DANNY: I said it first!

BRAD: I'm telling. Teacher, teacher! He said he's gonna take my truck.

TEACHER: Are you Mr. T?

BRAD: I'm Hannibal.

DANNY: Can I be Hannibal, Mr. T?

BRAD: Sure. I'm Mr. T, you're not. You're Hannibal.

DANNY: Sorry sorry sorry sorry sorry. Come on, man.

BRAD: Want to get the car? Race car.

DANNY: Mine goes like that. Hold it, man.

Working together—Michael and Matthew are actively helping now—
they gradually construct an identifiable vehicle out of a line of blocks.
Mr. T drives what turns out to be the space shuttle. "Bombs" made
of Lincoln logs are inserted into the hollow at the rear.

MICHAEL: Where do I sit?

BRAD: No, no! That's my smoke thing. There's fire in there, see?
This is going to be the smoke thing. Danny, Danny. Put it right
here. Hammer it.

MICHAEL: It'll burn you.

DANNY: He's our friend. Let him on. (*Matthew has arrived. He
sits down.*)

MICHAEL: That's gonna burn you!

MATTHEW (*hastily standing up*): Ow!

Zach and Warren arrive. They try to sit down. Michael tells them to
get out, and they appeal to the teacher. "That's hot there, watch
out," she says.

This teacher's words connect children with the rules of the play
script rather than the rules of the classroom, encouraging them to
devise solutions for themselves. "That's hot there, watch out!" If you
pay attention, maybe you can find a place on the space shuttle. "Are
you Mr. T?" in response to "Teacher, teacher! He said he's gonna take
my truck," reminds the player of his role rather than trying to solve the
dispute. The adult facilitator takes the play script seriously and helps
the children sustain it.

INTERRUPTING TO TEACH CONCEPTS

The interruption of play also happens in the name of cognitive
stimulation; the teacher intervenes to teach vocabulary and concepts.

Adults who have learned that play should be taken seriously some-times try to adapt it to their own idea of what's serious.

> At Second Street child care center, Ebony is playing in the block area as her teacher watches.
> EBONY: Watch this. (*She rolls a car down the ramp.*)
> TEACHER: Ebony, is that the freeway?
> EBONY: Yeah. Watch this, teacher!
> TEACHER: Is your car going down? Is it going down the freeway ramp? Is it going fast? How many cars do you have? Is your car going up again? Ebony, can you answer my question?
> No, Ebony isn't interested in the teacher's questions. She is absorbed in her play, until Marina grabs the ramp. Ebony squeals.
> TEACHER: Marina, Ebony had it first. You drive your car there. It needs to go in the same direction. (*Marina tentatively pushes her car down the ramp after Ebony's car. Ebony doesn't mind.*)
> MARINA: Look at me. Look at me. Look at my car. (*No one responds.*)

These are young 3-year-olds, and their language is fairly limited. The adult's intent was to stimulate more complex language—but, as often happens, the adult's language was all that could be heard. After asking, "Ebony, is that the freeway?" she asked five more questions in rapid succession, introducing up and down, freeway and ramp, and how many, all at once. "Ebony, can you answer my question?" she finally insisted. No way. Ebony's interest was in her car—"Watch this"—not in answering questions, and the teacher's intended facilitation fell flat. The teacher thought she was using power *for*, but power is defined by its outcomes, rather than its intent. It is defined from the child's point of view (Trook, 1983).

Perhaps Ebony just didn't want to talk. But she had initiated the conversation, with "Watch this, teacher!" Here are some possible alternative dialogues.

> EBONY: Watch this.
> TEACHER: Ebony, is that the freeway?
> EBONY: Yeah. Watch this.
> TEACHER: I'm watching. It goes fast, doesn't it?
> EBONY: Yeah. It go real real fast. Want to watch it again?
> TEACHER: Can you make it go faster?
> EBONY: Yeah. Real real fast. Lookit! I pushed it HARD.

EBONY: Watch this.
TEACHER: Ebony, is that the freeway?
EBONY: Yeah. Watch this.
TEACHER: Your car is going down the freeway.
EBONY: My car is going fast down the freeway. There it go!
TEACHER: It's going really fast. That's a fast car.
EBONY: That MY fast car.

In both these dialogues the teacher experiments with descriptions of the car and its action. In each, Ebony expands her vocabulary in response to the teacher's suggestions, which are offered within Ebony's own agenda—"Watch!"—and respond to the action of the moment: The car is going fast.

This teacher is eager to think about her interactions with children; she was actively interested in the alternative dialogues that the observer suggested. "Come again, won't you?" she asks, "and bring the video camera. If we have a video, we can watch it together later."

When the video day arrives, she has decided to use block play again, this time with dinosaurs and zoo animals, to "teach position words"—under and over, top and bottom and side—in support of the lesson plan she has written for the week.

TEACHER: What could we do with them? He's got a long neck.
VICTOR: Look at my long one.
TEACHER: Does that one fit under the bridge? . . . Look at Jerry, he's got his dinosaur on top of his head. Let's see if I can put mine on top of my head. Look, it fell down.
JERRY: You can't reach my dinosaur.
TEACHER: I can't reach your dinosaur. Let me try. . . . The cow is inside of the bus. . . . He's driving on top of my legs. Want me to make a bridge with my legs? Then he can go underneath my legs.
ANNIE: He's going to jail.
TEACHER: Why?
ANNIE: Because he got beat up. (*Victor zooms along with a speeding fire truck. Several children join the fire theme.*)
TEACHER: What is that car doing there? Looks as if it's riding on top of my knee.

Later the teacher and observer watch the video together and talk about it. "I had in my plans to teach position words, so that's what I did in the block area. I think maybe I used too many, though; one or two would have been enough," the teacher explains.

The observer responds, "I could hear you 'underlining' them as you said them. I was interested to see how your plan gave you the reason to be in the blocks and stay there. The children liked having you there. The video shows, though, that sometimes your words fostered not sustained play but 'Look at me, teacher.' Putting dinosaurs on top of heads was fun, but it didn't take the play anywhere. Look, there's Jerry putting it back on his head and asking you to look at him. He's more interested in your attention than in playing."

The teacher agrees. "But what about my lesson plans?" she asks.

The observer asks, "Could you keep them in mind and look for opportunities to use position words in context? When Annie drove her plane up to the block arch, your spontaneous question, 'Will it go *under* the bridge?' was her question too, and you put it in words for her. At that moment, *under* was part of the play sequence; it was language in context."

The teacher laughs, "Oh, and that's what was happening at snack time. We had fruit cocktail, and the children started looking for the grapes. I remembered to bring in position words: 'Where was your grape? Was it at the bottom?'"

The observer says, "And the children used the words too, because the position of the grapes was part of the game. In the block play, you used position words but the children didn't. Their agendas were dinosaurs and jail and fire, not inside and down."

Lesson plan objectives that are as specific as this one are apt to lead teachers into inappropriate behavior. If objectives must be written, the adult can try for something like, "Children will talk during their play." Such general objectives alert teachers to observe children's behavior while retaining role options for themselves. If children are talking as they play, the teacher can watch without intervening. If they aren't talking, or if their vocabulary is monotonous, she might decide to enter into the action to complicate it and to encourage verbalization. Adult intervention in play should be designed to sustain it, not get it off track.

BUILDING ON CHILDREN'S PLAY

Attentive teachers can build on play in order to "engage children's minds," in Katz and Chard's (1989) phrase. Some teacher guidance during play can be preplanned, as in Shopping at Fedco (Chapter 4). At other times it comes out of on-the-spot judgments made by the teacher as mediator, as in the discussion of knives with the Ninja Turtles in Chapter 3, and in the following episode:

> On a day when the 4-year-old boys were suddenly running around the yard and through the house in wild, delightfully silly pursuit, seemingly oblivious to other children, doors, or the clatter they were generating, I stopped them after about five minutes. Since their rambling had not developed naturally into something with more of a purpose, I suggested they make a plan for their play.
>
> Geoffrey called it "Flight of the Rambos." I don't know if he had the idea before the running or as a result of it. To help them develop the context for this theme, I urged that we decide on a few rules for their play. The cardboard tubes they had were to be telescopes. And they wanted to build flying ships for themselves out of large hollow blocks. I asked several other questions, to help develop their thinking. What is the design for the flying ships? Will you need supplies for them? Who will play the navigator, and who will be the co-pilots? (Reynolds, 1988, pp. 88–89)

For two of the boys, this was an interruption; they left the play. For the rest, it was a welcome challenge to their competence in building, inventing, and cooperating.

> Geoffrey was doing a lot of verbal planning and cooperating, which was new for him. Ty gave up needing to be in control and engaged in mutual problem-solving. Fredy found the play to be so stimulating and fulfilling that he no longer needed to be silly. None of the children was excluded, and Brian was easily accepted in the role he had created for himself as a neighboring flyer.
>
> What delighted me was that after my initial assertion for a theme and some rules, the boys took over. They directed the entire scenario. (Reynolds, 1988, p. 89)

"The boys took over" is the criterion for the success of this intervention; it focused and extended, not destroyed, the play. In play, the children are in charge. Appropriate teacher intervention is open-ended, leaving the choice with the children. Play is always negotiable; adults set the limits within which it occurs, but children invent the play itself and the changing rules that govern it.

When in doubt, trust the play. It is the children's curriculum. Play that is scattered or potentially disruptive may require refocusing, but well-focused, complex play requires no intervention. It has its own rhythm and will come to its own conclusion. It takes place on the children's turf, on which the adult has no legitimate role.

Adults who interrupt play, whatever their reasons, are usually in so much of a hurry that they fail to pay attention to children's purposes. SLOW DOWN is advice to keep in mind. We shortchange young children when we hurry them. We learn most about them, and help them learn most, when we pay attention to what is happening for them as they play.

⑥ Teacher as Scribe

Many adults are helped to pay attention if they have a defined task that keeps their attention focused. Some teachers of young children spent their student teaching days with a pad and pencil in an apron pocket, ready to take anecdotal notes on children's behavior and turn them in to a supervisor or discuss them at a seminar. Some of them keep this habit throughout their careers, but others simply give it up. What would they do with all those notes, if they kept on taking them?

In this chapter and the next two, we suggest reasons for continued note-taking and for making other representations of children's play. These activities emphasize the teacher as collector and organizer of data—solid professional behaviors that challenge teachers' skills and encourage them to pay close attention to the content of children's play. One role that requires these behaviors is teacher as scribe.

In the days when most people didn't write, communities had scribes—professional writers who wrote down messages other people wanted to send. In groups of young children, most people don't write; they're just beginning to learn about the process. The adults in the group, who do write, can model the writing process by acting as scribes.

Reading, writing, and 'rithmetic, the basic skills taught in primary schools, are modes of representing human experience. Dramatic play is young children's mode of representing their experience; they are pretending to be and do many things. They play at "nurturing and guiding like a daddy or a mommy, presenting a story like a reader, planning and building carefully like a worker, taking the time to think and write a list like a shopper, sitting with your family like a newspaper reader, or acting with care and courage like a fire fighter" (Stadler, 1990, p. 42). They are representing their observations of adult behavior in their play. Pretend play is one of the stages of representation that culminate in literacy, the most abstract form of representation. Oral language, which young children are rapidly mastering, is another form of representation. Children are also practicing representation through their two- and three-dimensional constructions, creating paintings of houses, drawings of people, worms of play dough, and roads of blocks. Some children can recognize their names in print, and they may even write them, or pretend-write them.

REPRESENTING CHILDREN'S PLAY

Teachers observing children's play sometimes write notes representing what they see, to be used in their developmental summaries, parent conferences, and curriculum planning. These notes serve as communication to adults. Teachers can also make representations, both written and pictorial, of children's play and language as communication to the children.

Kelly is building a tower of large colored plastic blocks. In his second year of preschool at Jefferson East, Kelly still has trouble focusing on a task and making friends, but he is very aware of the printed word and of adults. His block towers are apt to tumble down on other people's heads. How could an adult help him focus on this task?

As Kelly builds, an observer tries drawing his tower on the nearby chalkboard. He is instantly alert. "What are you doing?" "I'm drawing your tower," answers the observer (see Figure 6.1a). "That's not right," insists Kelly, "they're a circle." The observer erases her rectangles and tries again, "Like this?" (See Figure 6.1b.) Kelly looks scornful, "No!" (But clearly he's interested in the challenge: How do you draw a cylinder?) The observer tries again, "Is this okay?" (See Figure 6.1c.) Yes, that will do.

Kelly keeps building. The observer keeps drawing. They admire each other's work. She writes, "Kelly built a building." Kelly tries to read it, "Kelly made that blocks." She crosses out "built a building" and writes his words. Kelly points, "That's the top of it. This is the floor." She writes his words (see Figure 6.1d).

Kelly does some more building, including a row of triangles, which the observer draws (see Figure 6.1e). Without noticing the drawing, he runs over to the play dough. Julio takes over the chalk and chalkboard for the next 15 minutes, but he doesn't erase the triangles. Ten minutes later Kelly glances over. "Hey! He drew my triangles!"

A week later when the observer returns, Julio is building a tower with the same blocks. Again the observer tries drawing it—on paper this time, because the block builders are in the way of the

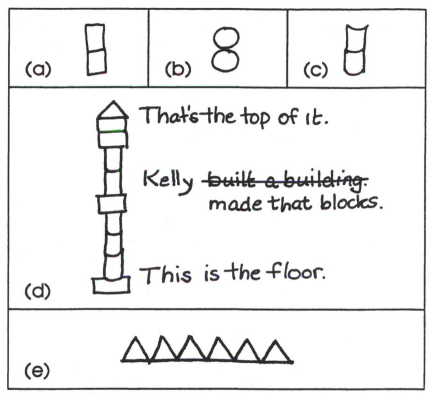

(a)

(b)

(c)

(d) That's the top of it.

Kelly ~~built a building.~~ made that blocks.

This is the floor.

(e)

FIGURE 6.1. "Kelly Made That Blocks"

chalkboard. She draws the outline with a marker and then decides to use crayons to color the blocks to match Julio's.

And here is Susana, wanting paper too. Susana draws Julio's tower, recognizably. She shows it to the observer, who asks, "Do you want to color it?" Yes, she does, and the observer gets crayons and more paper for Susana and for two other girls who want to draw too.

Susana shows her colored drawing to the observer. "Do you want to write your name?" the observer asks. Yes, she does, with a string of letters along the bottom of the page.

Julio has enlisted help from Sandra, the teacher, to steady his tall, tall tower. He's standing on a chair to build it higher. DOWN it falls. Sandra sympathizes and invites him to build it again. She shows him the drawing of it that the observer has laid on the floor nearby.

At first he doesn't recognize it. Then, suddenly, he gets it. He takes it and holds it up to show the other block builders. "Look, you guys! It's my tower. Build it like this." They get to work, and he puts the drawing down to join them. The observer and the teacher exchange delighted glances. "May I tape it up here?" asks the observer. She puts it on the wall.

Susana has been busy drawing. She has drawn the tower twice more, on new sheets of paper, and again written her "name" along the bottom. The observer tapes up her drawings too.

Just as children can discover that their words, spoken, make print, Julio has discovered that his block building can make a picture. And a picture can be used to tell someone else how to build it. That's a good thing to know. Meanwhile, Susana has observed the observer-as-scribe and tries on this role for herself, effectively and with concentration. Playing-at-being-an-adult-who-writes (or draws) is an absorbing activity for many children. It is helpful to children to offer them models of adults in this kind of action.

SHARING REPRESENTATIONS WITH CHILDREN

It doesn't take much drawing skill to sketch a block tower. But Theresa, another teacher, has real drawing skill and likes to use it, as part of her own playfulness in teaching. One day she made this observation in her preschool classroom.

> In the house area a group of children gathered using the telephones. Rosa was talking to the doctor: "Doctor, mi niña está muy enferma."
>
> On the side of the house area were Juan, Joanie, Yolanda, Alex, and Diana. They had dressed up with clothes from the house area and sat in a row of chairs, one in back of the other. Yolanda was driving the "train." There were plastic crates that were hauled from the block area; Yolanda put all her belongings in the crates, and then all the other children on the train did too.
>
> The children played for about 15 minutes. Then suddenly they all dispersed to different areas. It was interesting to see how they carried on without an adult.
>
> (Theresa Barrios, teacher/observer)

Theresa drew the picture in Figure 6.2 to go with her written observation, sketching it quickly and then finishing it after school. The

FIGURE 6.2. "Mi Niña Está Muy Enferma"

next day she brought it to circle time. "Do you know what I saw yesterday?" she asked the children. "I saw Rosa talking to the doctor on the telephone. 'My baby is very sick,' she told the doctor. And I drew a picture of her. Do you see her?" Theresa held up the picture and the children squeezed close to see. "Rosa," they said. "Con el teléfono." Rosa, overwhelmed, put her hands over her face. Yolanda, who had been looking closely at the picture, burst out, "That's me! I driving!"

"Yes, that's Yolanda," agreed the teacher. "Yolanda and Juan and Diana and Alex and Joanie went on the train. And here they are." There was great excitement. Our teacher drew our picture, and there we are!

At the end of circle time there was a rush for the crates and chairs. Reminding children of their interesting play encourages them to repeat it, to understand and elaborate it more fully.

Young children in a group can talk, briefly, about what they've been playing, but their talk generally lacks the richness of detail that characterized the play itself. And children find it hard to listen to each other in a large group; the teacher is more practiced in holding the attention of an audience. By using her own representations of children's play, she can stimulate children's oral language as well as their understanding that play can be represented on paper. This teacher is indeed teaching, while acknowledging the importance of the children's play and deriving her teaching directly from it. Children are most likely to understand representation when it mirrors their own actions.

> Today the observer who likes drawing block buildings is at Second Street child care center, with the 4-year-olds. A good many children are absent because of chicken pox, and the teacher is more available to individual children than she is sometimes able to be. She is helping Edward and Richard build a structure with the hollow blocks and boards; it's as tall as her head, but she's keeping it safe.
>
> "It's a Totally Hidden Video," says Edward, explaining and demonstrating how it works. The holes in the blocks, all lined up, are just right for looking through a camera. Edward takes his teacher's picture ("ch ch ch ch ch" says the camera), and Kathy's too, when she comes over from the art table to see what's going on.
>
> "Do you have a real camera?" the observer asks the teacher. "That's an amazing structure."
>
> "Yes, but no film," the teacher apologizes.
>
> "Maybe I'll draw it, then," says the observer, secretly delighted there's no film. Drawing offers more possibilities. She makes one, and writes a description on it. At clean-up time, when Richard is putting blocks away, the teacher says to him, "Richard, don't take the camera down. Leave the camera up. We would like to take a picture of everyone."
>
> The children have come together on the rug, where the teacher invites them to talk about their morning and writes their words with a marker. The aide tacks them up on a bulletin board so everyone can see (see Figure 6.3).
>
> It's Edward's turn to talk about his video. He demonstrates it. Then the observer is invited to share her drawing (see Figure 6.4).

I played blocks
with Edward.
For cars a bridge.
                                    Richard.

I played at the art table.
I made something for my mom.
                                    Katie

I played in the art area.
I colored. I played with
                                    animals.
Katie wanted to play animals.
And Richard. Then Mrs.
Kelly made a butterfly and
he got big.   Stephanie

FIGURE 6.3. What We Played This Morning

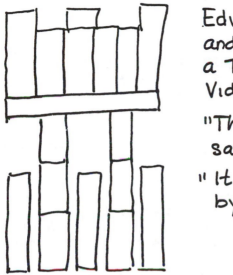

Edward and Richard and Mrs. Scott made a Totally Hidden Video.

"This is the picture," said Edward.

" It takes pictures by itself. "

FIGURE 6.4. "A Totally Hidden Video"

She does, reading the words. Edward looks at the picture critically: "This one isn't here." He points to the tall block at the upper right.

"You're right," says the observer. "I drew it and then you changed it. You know what I'll do? I'll change the picture. I'll cross out that block, like this." And she does.

Edward points to three more blocks in the picture that were removed from the structure during clean-up. The observer crosses them out too. Then they count the blocks across the top of the drawing to see if it's accurate now.

Edward has not only represented an idea he had; the observer has reproduced his representation in another medium, and he has "read" it, accurately. A thoroughly impressive accomplishment, when one is 4 years old.

When adults draw or write, they are models for children, who can try drawing and writing too. Some teachers photograph children in action, another mode of representation, and post or make books of the photos for children to look at and talk about. Pictures in any mode encourage reflection on experience. When adults take photographs, however, they're not modeling something children can do. (Children play with cameras, but there's no product.) Simple, clear drawings invite children to compare them with the original, to read the diagram, and to draw for themselves.

STIMULATING WRITING AS PLAY AND COMMUNICATION

There is also the written word, to be shared by adults and child writers. On another day at Second Street, an observer who sits down at the outside table with her pen and yellow pad finds herself surrounded by would-be writers.

> STEPHANIE: I want to help you. What are you doing?
> OBSERVER: I'm writing about children playing.
> STEPHANIE: Could I have some of your paper, please? (*The observer gives her a sheet of paper and a pen.*) I'm going to write about children playing, too.

Soon there are five children writing (the observer is relieved to find an accumulation of pens at the bottom of her purse). One makes very accurate letters; one invents cursive script. All seriously tackle the task, in their own ways. They are disappointed when it's time to go inside.

Returning the next week, the observer brings along a writing toolbox to be shared. Stocked with paper, used envelopes, pens and pencils, staplers and tape and scissors, it enjoys instant popularity. Six children are already engrossed in creating with the materials when the teacher comes up with a crying Richard by the hand. He is sad about his mother's departure and has been crying for some minutes.

The teacher invites him to join in the activity: "Here's some yellow paper. Write Mommy a note and tell her you miss her." Pointing to the container, she asks, "Would you like to choose a pen?" Then, "We'll give Mommy the note when she comes to pick you up this afternoon."

Literacy gives power. Richard stops crying immediately, though he continues to look sad. He clutches the pen high above the point, making letters and letter-like forms. The teacher sits close to him.

When he has stopped writing, she asks, "Richard, do you want to tell me about this?" Richard doesn't respond, so she continues, "Want me to write something down?" She waits a bit, but he is still silent. "Is this to Mommy? Want me to write that down?" Richard nods, and the teacher writes "To Mommy." "What else do you want to say?" she asks. When no response is forthcoming, she suggests, "Want to think about it?'

She gives the pen back to him, and he writes a bit more. Then, in a quiet voice, he starts speaking to the observer seated across the table from him:

"I got a balloon at my house.
The air is coming out.
It's blue.
While I was asleep.
While I was eating cereal. Lucky Charms cereal.
I have apples at my house. And oranges.
My house is blue.
And pears."

He shows the observer two tiny, recognizable drawings he has made with the pen on a large sheet of paper: "That's my pear right here. And this is my apple."

Again, the children are playing at being writers, enjoying the power that it gives them to be like, and to communicate with, adults—even absent mommies. It is the action of writing, not the product, that is important, though Stephanie shows the observer her carefully printed "OREO" and Richard, after leaving the table, comes back to get his letter to Mommy and put it safely in his cubby. Adults, who have mastered writing, may choose from time to time to use writing products to remind children of words they have said and plans they have made, in the process also demonstrating that writing is talking written down.

WRITING CAN BE READ

At Jefferson East preschool, Irma, the aide, has just read the children a homemade book about a turkey hunt and has told them they can look at it during play time. Now the children are planning together before they go off to play, in two groups, with the teacher and the aide. The adults have big sheets of paper and markers.

> TEACHER: I'm going to write a name. (*She writes "Barbara."*)
> BARBARA (*recognizing her name*): Irma's book.
> TEACHER (*writing*): Barbara—to see Irma's book. (*Adding, as Barbara talks*) Turkey. About the man. (*Continuing to the next child*) Luis.

LUIS (*recognizing his name*): En la cocina—con comida.

KELLY: That's not *my* name. What's *cocina*?

TEACHER: A kitchen. (*She continues writing the children's names and choices.*)

KELLY: In the playhouse.

TEACHER: Do you know what you're going to do in the playhouse? Have you decided?

KELLY: I'm gonna cook. (*The teacher writes his words.*)

SUSANA: A jugar con los bloques de colores.

KELLY: What is *colores*?

TEACHER: *Colores* is *colors*.

The list is complete. As the teacher reads it aloud, the children move off to their play—except for Luis and Karl, who are more interested in the planning list. Luis, who is 5 years old and can write his name, uses the teacher's marker to add writing of his own to the list and to circle some letters and words. When he's finished, the teacher asks him to take it to the art table, where she invites Karl to have a turn. Karl can't write yet, but he spontaneously practices circling words at random, making circles, and drawing on his hand. Learning to write takes lots of practice, of many kinds.

After clean-up time the children join Irma on the rug as they're ready. The teacher arrives with the planning lists, which she puts on the floor in front of her. The children are a close, interested group as she reads down the list. "Did you play with the blocks, Susana?" she asks. "Did you play with the train, Julio? No? Okay."

It is clear to the children that this is functional print; it gives the teacher messages. Some of them are looking at her; some of them are looking at the print themselves, finding their names and their friends'.

Later, when the children are outdoors, Kelly comes over to Irma to show her his sand pie, neat in its shiny pie pan. The teacher, nearby, writes down his words as he speaks (see Figure 6.5). Kelly turns and sees the big sheet of paper with his name on it. "What's that?" he asks, to which the teacher responds, "Can you read that?" "Yes," he says, "Kelly." She reads the rest to him, pointing out the words. When she reads "three cherries," he says, "Four cherries."

(Sandra Rangel, teacher/observer)

In this preschool Kelly and Luis, who are among the oldest children, are most curious about writing. In any program a few 3-year-olds, some 4-year-olds, and many 5-year-olds will be actively interested in the written word. Dianna, who teaches kindergarten, is more

kelly said, "Irma, I made a pie.
       Cherry pie.
       One cherry.
       Two cherries.
       Three cherries
       Four cherries."

FIGURE 6.5. "Four Cherries"

systematic than Sandra in preschool in scribing children's words and reading them back. Dianna tells this story (Ballesteros, 1988):

One day we offered bubbles as a choice at the back table. When the six children choosing that center arrived to play, conversation burst (and we wrote down their words).

You can stack them.
The bubbles.
You can build with them.
Put one of yours on top of mine.
On the table.
See they stick together.
Yours is bigger.
We made a bubble cave.
I have a tiny bubble.
I have a row of bubbles.
One big bubble.
Double bubble.
She's got a triple.
Oh oh. Ooooh!
How did you do that?
Can we take them home?

At group time, these words-written-down are introduced by the teacher to the children: "Did you know you made a bubble poem?" She reads it to them. Then she writes, "Bubbles, Bubbles, Bubbles" at the top and asks, "Do you know what this word says?"

Virgil said, "The bubbles."
Cassandra said, "I love bubbles."
  Lizzy said, "Double bubble."
 Caitlin said, "Triple bubble."
 Rafael said, "We made a bubble cave."
  Jorge said, "I love bubbles."
We all said, "Bubbles, bubbles, bubbles."

FIGURE 6.6. "Bubbles, Bubbles, Bubbles"

"Bubbles!" "Do you see the word 'bubbles' anywhere else on the page? Would someone like to come up here and take a crayon and make a circle—a bubble!—around one of the bubble words?"

Here's an exciting challenge for some of the children, and plenty of turns. (You can put more than one circle around a word, they decide.) Then they read it again, the teacher pointing to the words so everyone can shout "bubble!" each time they get to one.

The bubble poem stays up on the wall, where children can look at it as they choose. The next day they read it together again. "Who was playing with the bubbles?" asks the teacher, and she writes down the names of the six children as they identify themselves. "Now, see if you can remember one thing you said about the bubbles. Caitlin?"

Caitlin wants more time to think. Virgil volunteers. "The bubbles."

The teacher writes: "Virgil said, 'The bubbles.'"

Cassandra: I love bubbles.

Those words don't seem to be in the poem, but that doesn't matter, and the teacher doesn't mention it. They're Cassandra's words, and the teacher writes them. Pretty soon she has written the phrases shown in Figure 6.6.

This teacher-as-scribe is building serious reading lessons on the active play of 5-year-olds. "Bubbles" is a word both memorable in experience and distinct in its shape as a word. Wetly real bubbles will continue to be available in the classroom, as will the word that represents them. And the children will keep learning both about the properties of bubbles and about the properties of words.

As children gain mastery of play, the role of teacher as scribe becomes more appropriate than the role of teacher as player. Children's capacity for dramatic play is accompanied by increasing capacity for representational drawing and construction, and interest in the modes of representation, including writing, used by adults. Scribed representations of children's play can stimulate a debriefing process in which children and adults encounter each other on the shared turf of mutual curiosity. What happened? Let's remember it, and look at it, and talk about it.

7   Teacher as Assessor and Communicator

Teachers are responsible for teaching. They are also responsible for assessing the growth of children and communicating their assessments to parents and school personnel. Developmentally appropriate assessment relies on observations of children's behavior made by the person who knows them best in this setting, their teacher. Ongoing observations provide a much more adequate sample of behavior than any test for young children. They permit focus on children's abilities, not disabilities—what the child can and does do, rather than on what she has not yet mastered.

How do teachers know what to observe? They try to look for individual children's strengths—both interests and skills, since skill learning comes out of the pursuit of interests—and to systematize observations over time so no child is missed. There will be more notes on some children than others, but each child has a record, extending over time and mapping growth in all its variability. The record includes teacher representations—photographs, drawings, and written words—of children's play, language, and constructions with nonexpendable materials (Kuschner, 1989; New, 1990), as well as samples of children's work—paintings, drawings, and writing. For example, one kindergarten teacher (Meade-Roberts, 1988) includes in each child's portfolio a monthly sample of the roll sheet on which she asks the children to sign in every morning. This enables her to see the successive approximations of their names, as in the development of Marco's "signature":

September: ∧⋁

November: M◊

March: M∧Яс◊

ASSESSMENT AS PART OF PLANNING

Assessment is an essential part of curriculum planning. But the assessment by standardized tests that dominates American public education beyond preschool is external to the teacher's planning process. Instead, it becomes *her* final exam: Have the children learned what the test makers say she should have taught them? (Kamii, 1990, p. 15). Understandably, many school administrators respond to this system by requiring teachers to "teach to the test"—to design their curriculum as cramming-for-exams (Jones, 1987). Even preschool teachers may feel some pressure to do the same, if the kindergartens that their children will attend screen entering children for their knowledge of shapes, colors, numbers, and letters.

To be an integral part of the planning process, assessment must be designed by teachers themselves to contribute to their knowledge of each child's growth in understanding. Goals, set by each program, should be developmentally appropriate, including attitudes and dispositions as well as knowledge and skills (Bredekamp, 1991). Informal and systematic observation during independent activity, including play, is the primary assessment tool in early childhood education.

Among one teacher's goals for her 5-year-olds is the acquisition of fine-motor skills. She observes systematically during play time.

> Each day we note a child's approach to tasks and his first choice of activity. For many weeks I noticed that Adrian never chose to work with scissors, crayons, or markers. The drawings in his journal were lightly marked, random crayonings. It was becoming clear to me that Adrian needed to practice doing some of the things he steered clear of. Since Rosa Linda, the instructional aide, and I agreed that Adrian needed to be taught to cut, she sat with him one morning, and without passing judgment because he couldn't use scissors, she showed him how. After that he practiced whenever he chose to; I never singled him out again for "cutting." By the year's end Adrian could cut, usually quite accurately. (Meade-Roberts, 1988, p. 96)

The teacher is able to observe Adrian's fine-motor skills, as well as his skills in building with blocks, making friends, and using language to meet his needs, because she has set the stage. As the basic elements in her curriculum, she (1) provides a physical environment full of many different things appropriate for 5-year-olds to do, (2) offers choices among all those different things, and (3) schedules the day for extended periods of choice. By giving Adrian permission to play, she has freed herself to observe him. Observing, she values the choices he makes and is able to note both his strengths and the areas in which she may need to challenge him.

Teachers also plan challenges for small groups of children. Play time is balanced by what is called "committee time" in some programs, 20 to 30 minutes during which a heterogeneous, continuing small group of children "is given a task to do within the confines of one center. There are many activities planned that cover a wide ability range, and the children use materials that are open-ended (blocks, for example). It is hoped that they will learn to work with one another, depend on one another and help one another in a small group setting" (Stritzel, 1989, pp. 24–25). The teacher chooses these activities based on his observations of children at play; having assigned them, he can interact or observe in any of the same roles he adopts during play time.

When teachers are free to choose where to begin observing, they often begin, sensibly, with their nonthrivers (Prescott, Jones, Kritchevsky, Milich, & Haselhoef, 1975) and the implicit question, What can I do about this child?

CAN I LEARN TO APPRECIATE HIM MORE?

At Second Street preschool on days when the teacher can count on the help of one or two experienced parent volunteers, she sometimes frees herself to observe during play time. She uses observation to try to get to know a child better. If there's a child she's having difficulty with, she explains, that may determine her focus, as it did one morning.

> Jimmy and Thomas had been driving us crazy with their out-of-bounds behavior at group and clean-up times. That morning, Jimmy ran out the door. When he was retrieved and sat at a table, he angrily pushed everything off the table. He was sucking his thumb as play time began. I had been intending to observe him, but I decided I was too frustrated by him, so I began watching Thomas instead. But it wasn't long before I was observing Jimmy too. Here's what I recorded.
>
> 8:55 Thomas has been wandering for 5 minutes. Now he disappears into the corner behind the cubbies.
> 9:05 No Thomas for 10 minutes! Oh, here he is. He's gone again. I peek into the corner to see what he's up to. He's putting puzzles neatly(!) back on the shelf and looking to see what else is there. He gets out the Legos.

9:10 Sarah approaches his corner; I can't see what she's doing, but Thomas yells "Stop!" I say to Sarah, "I think he wants to play with that by himself." Sarah takes some beads over to a table, leaving Thomas alone.

9:15 Jimmy (where's he been?) runs over to Thomas. He gets some Legos and now both are building, next to each other and talking. They're nice and cozy.

9:25 Oh oh, they've made guns. "Freeze up, everybody," says Jimmy, moving out into the room. "Freeze up, everybody," says Thomas, following. "We have guns," says Thomas to the aide. "No," she says, "we don't have guns at school." (But they already do! Do I talk like that too?) "You can make a rocket ship or maybe a car." I wonder what will happen. It's hard, but I'm going to stick to my observer role and not say anything right now . . . will wait and see.

9:30 They're both back in the corner with the Legos. "I have a gun," Jimmy says to no one in particular. He gets down an alphabet puzzle and works it. Quiet conversation between Thomas and Jimmy, with Thomas piecing together Legos next to Jimmy doing puzzle.

9:35 T. and J. have wandered out of the Legos. Jimmy is watching other children doing string-painting. Thomas is shooting his gun in the blocks. To me: "I made this gun myself." I manage to say, "You made that gun yourself." He wanders off with his gun, shooting now and then, talking to himself. Jimmy runs over to him: "Gimme my gun!" Thomas defends *his* gun and Jimmy runs back to the Legos corner. He starts digging through the box of Legos for the pieces he wants.

9:40 Jimmy has been intent on Legos for several minutes now. Thomas looks around for him and when he sees J. at the Legos, T. joins him. Now they are side by side again, both piecing together Lego "guns," intently. Wow! Look at that! Jimmy hands T. a piece from his own pile. More intent building by both. Aide has either decided to ignore or she has forgotten; she is busy with the easel painting. Maybe she is confused by my response?

9:47 Clean-up bell. Now Thomas is roaming and shooting. Jimmy and two girls have joined him with Lego guns.

9:50 Jimmy comes away from Legos with a complicated gun. Part of it falls off. "See, you stupid!" he yells as he gets down on the floor to fix it. "Me?" asks one of the girls. "No, the other girl," says Jimmy. He repairs the gun and goes to find Thomas. It falls apart and he fixes it in the blocks.

9:55 Some kids are really cleaning up. Aide is. I'm too busy watching. Jimmy and Thomas are still carrying guns about.

10:00 Aide: "Ok, everyone, come sit in the circle." Most kids do.
Thomas is working on his gun. He starts to put it away, takes it
out to fix it again, then puts it carefully on the shelf and starts
toward the circle. He meets Jimmy, who has a stethoscope.
Thomas tries to grab it and aide takes it away. Both boys pick
up long blocks for guns and roam the edge of the circle.
"Teacher!" says Sarah. They are disarmed.

Written later: When I said, in circle, "We need to see if our
room is clean. How about the Lego table?" Jimmy responded immediately. It was his corner, and he went back to check it. He put a
block away as he came back. "Who's a good block fixer?" I asked.
"Me!" said Jimmy. "You had a lot of turns. Someone else," I said. I
think that was a mistake; since then Jimmy kept disturbing and
couldn't settle until the aide took him on her lap, saying, "If you're
going to be my helper you need to sit right here." Bless her. He relaxed onto her lap with pleasure and joined Five Little Monkeys
wholeheartedly.

What I learned: Thomas played for an HOUR and Jimmy for 40
minutes, mostly in serious construction with Legos. They were able
to be friends and do dramatic play. It was gun play, which is against
the rules, but they used their guns to swagger with, not to bother
others. I'm glad I didn't stop them; they worked hard and well at
those guns, and I think they need them for protection. Neither finds
preschool a comfortable place to be yet. I think I like them better
than before.

Focused observation enabled this teacher to understand, much
better than she had, two children whose behavior she usually found
troublesome. She discovered some real strengths in their absorbed
playing and parallel dramatic play, which included cooperation
and conversation as well. They were enjoying being together and
having private space to work in. These were 3-year-olds who received a lot of necessary power *on*; here they were inventing ways to
be powerful. Watching them, the teacher got interested in their play.
She moved past her pressing management question—What can I do
about this child?—to child-centered questions: What interests him?
What issues is he dealing with? What does he know? What might he
learn next?

BUILDING ON A CHILD'S STRENGTHS

A teacher who understands children better is, indeed, likely to like them better. And she can communicate her feelings to parents, some of whom are also puzzled and frustrated by their children. At Jefferson preschool Kelly's mother has told his teacher of her impatience with his behavior toward his little brother and toward the children next door. Kelly wants very much to make friends, the teacher has observed, but other children often reject him. In his disappointment he looks for someone or something to knock around.

Kelly's teacher too is often exasperated by him. She has had to make a conscious effort to observe his behavior at its best, looking for strengths that might serve him in building the relationships he craves. His active interest in the written word is something she is able to appreciate and capitalize on, in her own relationship with him and in planning activities to challenge him and some of the other 4-year-olds.

The activity described below was stimulated in part by her observations of Kelly's, Luis's, and Barbara's interest in writing. As she participated in it, she was able to gather more observational data on their development of competence.

On a previous day the children made drawings with chalk on purple construction paper. These have been laminated as book covers, with sheets of plain paper bound between. The teacher hands them out to the children, one by one, as they sit on the rug together.

TEACHER: Kelly, here's yours.

KELLY: Thanks!

TEACHER: You're welcome.

KELLY: Does it have papers in it?

TEACHER: What could you do with it if it has papers in it?

KELLY: You could write in it. (*He explores it, pleased.*)

TEACHER: Now we're going to go to the tables and we're going to make pictures in the books and maybe we can write in them. OK?

The tables are set up with new boxes of crayons, and pencils and pens. The adults sit with the children, available to write words if asked.

KELLY: I made a hurricane.

TEACHER (*writing*): Kelly made a hurricane. (*Kelly reads it.*)

LUIS: Can you make a car?

TEACHER: I'll write *car* for you. Where do you want me to write *car*?

SUSANA: Teacher! I wrote my name.

BARBARA (*drawing on every page with crayon and "writing" on every page with pen*): I wrote my name too.

LUIS: I'm making numbers! Teacher, look at my numbers.

KELLY: There's my race track.

TEACHER: Want me to write?

KELLY: Kelly made this race track. How do you write *race track*?

TEACHER: I'll show you.

KELLY: I want a longer one. (*He enlarges the period she has made.*) This is another race track.

Luis is now making numbers for Kelly.

KELLY: Zoo. Kelly made a zoo. This is a race track in a zoo. (*He scribbles. Then he carefully writes an O—"and a Z," he says.*) This is a race track in a zoo.

LUIS: This is a race track in a zoo.

KELLY (*coloring with a whole handful of crayons*: Luis! Look, Luis!

LUIS: Teacher, lookit. I made a door. And a house. And a car. . . . And a motorcycle in the house. It went brr brrm. . . . I'm not finished.

Drawing, scribbling, writing, and oral language absorb all the children for 20 minutes. Toward the end, Kelly disappears under the table, where Barbara and Luis join him. The other children continue to work. Then Kelly reappears: "I'm back. I'm not invisible anymore."

(Sandra Rangel, observer)

WHO IS THIS CHILD?

Observation during play time permits attention to the uniqueness of each child. Play and language, like image-making and writing, reflect what matters most to the child. To master writing, as a 6- to 8-year-old (and beyond), it is necessary to find one's voice (Ashton-Warner, 1963; Dyson, 1989; Graves, 1983; Johnson, 1987). To master play, as a 3- to 5-year-old, it is equally necessary to find one's voice, which is an aspect of self-concept development. The young children who are master players know who they are and are representing themselves through their play, as they will later do through their writing.

To help all children master play, teachers might well try Graves's (1983) advice for getting to know each child. In three columns:

1. Try listing from memory all the children in your class. (Then draw a line, and add below it those you have forgotten.)

2. For each child, list his or her experiences and interests.
3. For each interest, indicate whether and how you have specifically confirmed it for the child. How have you helped him/her to play it, talk about it, recognize it as valuable?

In Graves's (1983) words,

The ultimate object of the column exercise is to be able to fill in all three columns, to carry the *unique territories of information about the children in memory*. Those children for whom it is most difficult to come up with a territory of information are *those who need it most*. They are often the children who find it difficult to choose topics, to locate a territory of their own. They perceive themselves as nonknowers, persons without turf, with no place to stand. (pp. 22–23)

To locate a territory of their own, children need plenty of time to explore and choose. At Second Street child care center, the staff has been experimenting with extending the outdoor play time by having only half the 4-year-olds at a time go in for teacher-planned small-group activities. Indoors there's "less mess, less noise," the aide says, pleased. Outdoors children who have had plenty of time for physical activity start gravitating toward easels and table activities, where they spontaneously create shapes and colors, letters and numbers. There are long turns—two or three turns or even six—for painting, and if more room is needed, paper and paints can be put on the table too. The teacher is relaxed with only half the group to supervise.

> LARRY (*repeating shapes that look like D's*): I'm painting 4's.
> TEACHER: And *you're* 4. We have lots of 4's here. (*When he's through, she admires the colors in his painting.*) That kind of matches my sweater, doesn't it? It matches my socks too.
> VANESSA (*arriving*): I'm going to make two pictures, OK?
> The teacher prints "Vanessa" on the paper. Vanessa takes the marker and copies her name, with remarkable competence. Instead of painting, she continues to use the marker to write, then pretend-write, and finally fill up the page with swirls. It is clear, watching Vanessa, that Piaget is right: Children construct systems for themselves, including written language.
> LARRY (*very interested*): Why's she writing her name? She gonna write it again?
> TEACHER: She's practicing her name.
> LARRY: Can I practice my name too?

TEACHER: Yes, when she's done.

LARRY: You gonna help me? (*He goes off on a bike.*)

TEACHER (*naming letters with a highly motivated Vanessa*): That's
    fancy writing, huh?

Edward, who has been painting on the other side of the easel for a
long long time, is done, and the teacher invites Larry for his turn.
She prints his name. He takes the marker and experiments with the
marks it can make. Inspired by Vanessa, he tries making a few letter-
like forms, but then he discovers dots, counting as he makes a great
many of them. Then he begins making marks and naming them.

LARRY: This is my mommy. . . . No, that isn't my mommy. This is
    a spider.

TEACHER: Where's your mommy?

LARRY: I'm gonna make her. Here. . . . This is my bed. . . . This is
    my brother. . . . Mama.

It's clear to the teacher that Larry and Vanessa are in different
places developmentally with writing (see Figure 7.1). As she looks
around she can see a wide range of development and focus among
the eight children, who, by now, all seem to be drawing and painting.
Each is discovering patterns and practicing and elaborating them.
Each moves back and forth from more mature to less mature representations; Vanessa, she notices, is now joyously painting her hand
with magenta "blood" and then covering both hands with yellow,
making "gloves." With her painty hands she makes prints all over a
sheet of paper on the table.

Stephanie doesn't like paint on her hands, but she likes
Vanessa's good idea. She traces her hand with a marker. Vanessa
like that idea, and soon almost everyone is using markers to make
hands, tracing their own or drawing freehand. Richard tells the
teacher that his is a baseball glove. Edward's hands have four fingers
and a wrist. Vanessa's hands have five fingers; she has done a whole
page of them, with different colored markers. Now she closes each
with a line and adds feet to some! (See Figure 7.2.)

COMMUNICATING TO PARENTS
AND OTHER ADULTS

For an hour, these 4-year-olds were engaged in creating symbols,
spontaneously using paints and markers outdoors, making collages
indoors. As they worked, they talked. Because the collages were exploratory, requiring little adult help, the aide was free to write down

Vanessa

Larry

mommy spider
mama
brother
↑ bed

79

FIGURE 7.2. Hands

children's words, in English and Spanish. Thanks to his initiative, the walls of the classroom and hall are covered with children's art projects, photos of some of their activities, and their words. Together with their parents, children look for their names on the walls and can talk about what they've done. By putting scribed representations of children's play and language on the walls along with children's own representations, teachers give a direct message to parents and other visitors: These are the important things that happen here. Children are learning through their activities.

These teachers also anticipate possible criticism ("All they do here is play.") by posting analyses of what children are learning in each of the free choice areas. Figure 7.3 is an example from another teacher, Anne Solomon, who teaches kindergarten in California's Rocklin district.

In most kindergartens and some preschools teachers are expected to communicate their observations to parents in conferences or written reports. At Live Oak child care center each child has a notebook in which caregivers and parents write back and forth to each other about the child whose care they share. At Live Oak preschool teachers and practicum students write twice-yearly narrative reports describing children's physical, social, emotional, and cognitive development as observed at school.

The kindergartens at Second Street School used to have report cards on which teachers were required to rate each child's progress as satisfactory/unsatisfactory. Recently teachers participated in a year-long cooperative effort to create a developmental profile on which a child's growth can be traced in its natural progression, with no stage labeled unsatisfactory. Parents are pleased, and teachers are finding the profile useful in focusing their observations of children (Jones & Meade-Roberts, 1991; Meade-Roberts, 1988). Within its broad catego-

BLOCKS

- ROLE PLAYING: building a farm, a city, a school, a house and acting out the parts
- PROBLEM SOLVING: figuring out how to do something and experimenting w/the materials
- COOPERATIVE PLAY: working w/friends to make things together
- ORAL LANGUAGE: talking about what's being made and how it's made
- PATTERN: using blocks to build a fence, road or similar buildings
- REPRESENTATION: building something to look like something the child knows about
- PART TO WHOLE: seeing that individual blocks can be used to build something even larger
- MATCHING: making 2 roads of equal length - making 2 towers exactly alike
- CREATIVITY: creating one's own ideas
- SELF-ESTEEM: feeling good about what is created - pride in one's accomplishments
- MEASUREMENT: figuring out how many blocks are needed to make equal sides of buildings
- CLASSIFYING: in cleaning up children sort blocks according to similarities
- BALANCE: experimenting w/blocks to make things that don't have 1 side that falls over
- EXTENSION OF LITERATURE: creating something from a story that's been heard
- SHAPE & SIZE VOCABULARY: rectangle, square, triangle, long, short, etc.
- SIZE RELATIONSHIP: longer, shorter, long, longer, longest

ries—literacy skills, numeracy skills, curiosity and creativity, physical development, social skills, and ability to meet school and teacher expectations—a teacher can watch for children's progress toward his priority goals for their development: competence in (1) representation and (2) relationship. Under *representation*, he looks closely at language, dramatic play, construction and creation with materials, and developing literacy and numeracy. Under *relationship*, he is alert to children's caring for others as shown in communication, cooperation, empathy, and conflict resolution. Children who are responsible, thoughtful group members and confident, creative representers will be ready for whatever schooling comes next.

In classrooms where children all do identical projects, different learnings take place and different messages are communicated to parents. The walls reflect adult rather than child activity: "We are learning about bunnies [or fall, or St. Patrick's Day], and our teacher has cleverly cut out shapes for us to glue ears on [or has made a collection of pictures], to remind us of the theme she has chosen for us."

> An observer at Second Street child care center, visiting when the classroom has a rabbit in residence, is admiring posted representations by teacher and children. Above the cage is a list of the children's invented "Rules for Peter/Reglos para el conejo: Don't drop Peter the rabbit. Don't hide him. Don't put things inside the cage. Don't squeeze the water. . . ." Next to the rules is Stephanie's spontaneous painting of a large rabbit, with a small cage in the corner of the page.
>
> The substitute teacher complains to the observer, "These children get away with too much. I think they need to learn right and wrong. I'm used to teaching numbers and colors, but here they won't let us use patterns. Not even bunnies."
>
> "But look at Stephanie's rabbit," says the observer. "Isn't that a more rabbity rabbit than any teacher-made pattern?"
>
> "Well, maybe," says the substitute teacher. "But that Stephanie, she's smart. Most of the children can't do that, you know."

Because Stephanie's teacher respects each child's abilities to create his own representations, the substitute will remain frustrated. But she is not alone; many adults who work with children find joy in cutting out patterns and shopping for holiday decorations. That's what their teachers did, when they were children in school; now it's their turn to play teacher. Walls decorated with such things reassure other adults, including parents, that there's really curriculum here. Thoughtful communication is necessary to help adults understand children's need to make their own representations and see models of their own words.

COMMUNICATING TO CHILDREN

In classrooms where children's work all looks alike, the children are practicing their teacher's ideas. When we encourage children to create for themselves, they learn there are many ways of doing things. Take kites, for example. Sometimes teachers, who know what kites look like, cut out diamond shapes for all the children to glue tails on. But real kites do come in different shapes, and pretend kites can come in even more.

At Madison West preschool, Georgina Villarino decided to encourage divergent thinking by putting out all sorts of materials in the art area—paper in various shapes, paper plates, circles with holes, hearts, feathers, flowers, tissue paper strips, yarn—and then invite children to come one at a time, so they wouldn't copy each other. The splendidly divergent results, with children's words added, now fly on a large bulletin board, light blue above and green below (see Figure 7.4).

"Children really pay attention to a bulletin board like this," says Georgina. "They made it themselves, and it's easy to tell whose work is whose. They look for their names. They move chairs over to the bulletin board and stand on them and look at their words and touch their kites and talk about them. And they show their parents. The parents are beginning to believe we really teach the children here."

In the role of scribe, writing children's words for them to see, teachers take brief notes every day. In contrast, the notes Thomas and Jimmy's teacher was making at the beginning of this chapter prompted an awed visitor to ask, "Do you write this much very often?"

"Of course not," said the teacher. "I like to write, and so notetaking is fun for me. My friends think I'm crazy. But I rarely take that much time to observe, and if I did, what would I do with all those notes? This was desperation time. I really needed to know what was going on with those kids."

"So those notes were for you," observed the visitor. "You were making a child study for yourself."

How can we make a kite?

¿Cómo podemos hacer un papalote o cometa?

"Yes, and to share with my aide, and for a possible referral," explained the teacher. "But the quality of play I saw when I was paying attention convinced me that it's our expectations that need to be changed. It's only when we interrupt them that those boys get outrageous. They're very young, and they're not yet tuned in to our routines. Jimmy was eager to help, once he'd had time enough for the transition and realized what was going on. We can manage them just fine if we recognize what's going on for them.

"I even showed some of what I'd written to Thomas's mother, to let her know I was pleased with his long attention span. She was a bit concerned about so much gun play, and that gave us a chance to talk about what he watches on TV. So it wasn't just for me, after all."

This teacher, like others we've described, makes regular notes of children's language and posts them, along with children's paintings and drawings, on the wall. It's the parents and older 4-year-olds who are most interested, she finds; the 3-year-olds are still absorbed in exploring materials and creating their own symbols, including Lego guns. She finds that extra effort is required to represent the whole range of children's work, including dramatization, language, and constructions made of blocks or Legos or other materials that get put away rather than taken home (Kuschner, 1989).

Constructions can be saved and labeled for short periods of time; children can write their own "PLS SV" signs or dictate their words to adults. Since this preschool has both morning and afternoon groups, children often choose something to save for the other group to see. Suitably labeled—"Luz and Ben built this airport"—it awaits discovery by the other children, who are helped to read the sign, talk about it if they wish, and then add to it or dismantle it as they pursue their own ideas with the blocks (Olivia Rivera, personal communication, 1990). When children share a classroom with other children they never see, messages are important!

Communicating with children is a two-way process. Vanessa and Larry and their friends let their teacher know, by their action, what they know about writing and painting—and hands. The teacher followed up this activity by choosing to serve as the "memory" of the group (New, 1990, p. 8); on the day that followed, she reminded the children of what they had done and added her representations to theirs. Finding their "hands" irresistible, she decided to sustain this interest, moving into the role of teacher as planner of emergent curriculum (see Chapter 8).

ACCOUNTABILITY: HOW DO WE KNOW
THEY'RE LEARNING?

In many settings, neither teachers nor children have permission to play at school. Learning is serious; "let's get down to business." Parents and administrators, and many teachers, are skeptical if children are "only playing." Their common sense and the behaviorist theory that guides American education generate a view of teaching as engineering: "a structured process of shaping behavior according to predetermined specifications much as industrial work involved the shaping of raw materials into prespecified products" (Donmoyer, 1981, p. 14). Consistent with this imagery, behavior-modification approaches to teaching use the metaphor of the marketplace, a system based on payment rather than on giving. These methods "inevitably promote a dichotomy between work and play, or—more broadly—between doing something because one *has* to, and doing something because one *wants* to" (Franklin & Biber, 1977, p. 8).

In a society focused on technology and consumption, the popularity of this view is understandable. But popular wisdom and developmental theory are at odds. In reviewing the relative places of behaviorism and Piaget's constructivism in the history of psychology, Kamii (1985a) explains,

> All sciences begin by studying surface, observable, and limited phenomena, and by explaining them with mere common sense. It is not surprising that psychologists, too, began by studying behavior, which is observable and easier to study than complicated phenomena such as human knowledge and morality. Teaching by telling and rewards makes good common sense, but the time has come for educators to go beyond mere common sense. (p. 7)

In constructivist theory, Kamii explains, children learn by going through one level after another of being "wrong." Science, and education, develop in the same way. A developmental approach in early childhood education represents a more complex and inclusive theory of learning than does the engineering metaphor. It uses a growth metaphor, in which the teacher is not an efficient engineer but a *nurturer of play*—of the child's spontaneous action. This definition is nowhere found in familiar conceptions of teaching.

The teacher who would nurture play, then, has both a political and a moral obligation to be accountable to those unfamiliar with the rationale for this view of learning. While skepticism about the value of play is widespread, it is no accident that parents in those groups that have traditionally lacked power in our economic system are particularly concerned when teachers let children play. Their children have been ill-served in our schools, often by teachers who lacked belief in their ability to learn. "You teach my kid!" is an understandable and justifiable demand by any parent, and especially by those whose suspicion that their children are victims of institutional racism or classism is well founded (Clemens, 1983; Delpit, 1988).

Our emphasis on the teacher's roles of scribe, assessor, communicator, and planner is a response to these genuine concerns. We have found that teaching staff who share parents' concern about teaching children move with pleasure into the role of scribe, which clearly supports the development of literacy and keeps staff responsibly active during children's play. Scribed products serve as effective communication to parents and other adults. Attention to the development of literacy scripts, by making writing materials and books generously available and responding to children's play with them, further supports children's growth in the skills that matter most in schools.

The critical and divergent thinking that children practice in play and problem solving contribute significantly to the higher-level thinking skills they will later need in school, though this outcome may be more difficult to convince parents of, especially parents who value obedience and rote performance. Shirley Brice Heath (1983) describes the children of Roadville, a white working-class community, whose parents expect young children at home to listen to stories read from books, answer questions following the reading, and do workbook tasks. "Adults in Roadville believe that instilling in children the proper use of words and understanding the meaning of the written word are important for both their educational and religious success" (p. 60). However, books and stories are separate from the rest of life in Roadville, and families do not play with words or ideas.

Roadville children do well in the early years of school. They have learned the surface rules of the school game: Pay attention, do what you're told, and respect the written word. They are stumped, however, when asked to create or critique stories or respond to hypothetical questions.

Thus their initial successes in reading, being good students, following orders, and adhering to school norms of participating in lessons begin to fall away rapidly about the time they enter the fourth grade. As the importance and frequency of questions and reading habits with which they are familiar declines in the higher grades, they have no way of keeping up or of seeking help in learning what it is they do not even know they don't know. (Heath, 1983, p. 64)

Creating and critiquing stories and dealing with "what if?" questions are skills learned through play and playful dialogue. The play of 3- to 5-year-olds is a crucial developmental stage in children's continuing construction of knowledge and in their learning to learn. To be accountable for children's learning while nurturing their play, teachers need to respond thoughtfully and imaginatively to the expectations of others, while retaining their responsibility as curriculum decision makers.

8 Teacher as Planner

"Did you see what I put on the wall?" the teacher at Second Street child care center asks Richard and Edward. "My hands!" says Edward promptly, recognizing both his name and his drawings. Richard's "baseball glove" is there too, but Richard ignores it; he has spotted the real baseball glove the teacher has put on the shelf below, together with several pairs of gloves in different sizes. He tries it on. Edward puts on gloves with rabbit fur cuffs and strokes his cheek with them. Larry arrives. "Who did them?" he asks, pointing to a row of cut-out paper hands along the bottom of the bulletin board.

"I did," says the teacher. "I traced my hand, and I cut it out."
"Can I cut too?" asks Larry.
"Sure," says the teacher, pleased with his interest. Paper, pencils, and scissors are already on the table. Larry and Richard go off to practice cutting, which is challenge enough for them; hands are temporarily forgotten.

The teacher has lots of ideas for continuing with hands, though. A light projected against a sheet will offer opportunity for shadow play; she remembers fondly the animal shapes her grandpa used to make with hand shadows on her bedroom wall. Shadows can be made outdoors too. She also remembers the Mummenschanz mime troupe she once saw, with white- and colored-gloved hands moving against a black background. She is inspired by that memory to try lining the puppet stage with black paper and finding more gloves.

Her aide knows some American Sign Language; perhaps he can teach the children some signs. Outdoors, Vanessa was spontaneously painting her hands; that's another way to make gloves. Hands come in different sizes—and skin colors, too, without benefit of paint; what about photographing everyone's hands and playing matching games with the pictures and the real hands? As adults and children talk, and create, and compare, and question, they'll keep on learning together.

If the children are interested, their ideas and the teacher's will be integrated into an extended project derived from children's spontane-

ous play and image-making. Such projects challenge children's thinking and extend their play (Katz & Chard, 1989; New, 1990). The
outcomes are likely to be stimulating to everyone involved. But planning for play doesn't begin with projects, in which teachers set the
direction and sometimes, in their enthusiasm, take over. Planning is an
emergent process in which play has priority. The outcome is an emergent curriculum—one in which both adults and children exercise initiative and make decisions.

EMERGENT CURRICULUM

Any curriculum is the outcome of someone's choices among all the
things in the world that there are for children to learn. In an emergent
curriculum, the choices are made by the children and by the adults
who know them. However, an emergent curriculum is never built only
on children's interests. Teachers are people with interests of their own
that are worth sharing with children. By doing some things teachers
themselves like, they model knowledge and enthusiasms—even adults
keep on learning—and stay interested in teaching.

Values held for children's learning in the school and community,
the family and culture, help to determine curriculum content. Curriculum also emerges from the things, people, and events in the environment, and from all the issues that arise in the course of living together
day to day. Caregiving, expression of feelings, and resolving problems
and interpersonal conflicts are not interruptions to the curriculum;
they are basic curriculum.

"Lesson plans," written before the fact, are often required of
teachers by supervisors who wish to ensure that careful thought is
given to the activities provided for children. Any thoughtful curriculum is planned both to be responsive to where children are and to take
them somewhere, in the direction of agreed-upon goals. If a curriculum is preplanned toward behavioral objectives, it is typically linear,
with only one way to go. But learning, as it happens, is nonlinear,
diverging along unexpected paths as new connections are made. For
this reason a web is a better planning model than an outline. It leaves
plenty of space for add-ons at the inspiration of everyone involved.
(An example of webbing is presented under "Introducing a New
Theme" later in this chapter.)

Emergent curriculum planning relies heavily on observation, and
it is best represented after the fact. The teacher's objectives are broad
rather than narrowly specified. He makes no claim that he will teach
80% of the children to name eight colors by December 1—the sort of

behavioral objective that builds in plenty of room for failure by both teacher and children (Jones, 1983). Instead, he provides a choice-full environment where children, as they explore and play, will have many opportunities to, for example: (1) hear and use oral language, (2) explore varied art media, (3) see and discuss written words, (4) practice solving interpersonal problems, (5) acquire various physical skills, and even, if he thinks it is important, (6) notice the colors of different objects and hear the color names during conversations about these objects.

The teacher's preplanning thus includes the contents and organization of the physical environment and the time schedule, and the stories, songs, activities, and conversations to be included in each day, which are selected for about a week at a time with room for last-minute changes. Any themes to be emphasized may be indicated for several months or for a whole year, with the expectation that some unpredicted interests will emerge along the way. All planning is done based on an understanding of the program's broad goals. There is, however, an absence of "The children will learn ———" objectives. Instead, the children will have opportunities to do ———, and the teacher will learn by observing them and thus continue to plan thoughtfully for children's construction of knowledge based on their doing.

By providing materials and interactions in organized space and time, teachers enable the play to get started. They continue to pay attention to what children are actually doing and learning, modifying plans on the spot when necessary and responding to children's ideas and interests with spur-of-the-moment teaching. Exploration and physical action come first, and then mastery of play. It is when children are well established as competent players and group members that they are ready for challenges like the *hands* theme described above or the *snails* theme described below.

Teachers discover children's skills and interests during observations of play. In the role of planner, a teacher may focus on the environment as it supports play or on the play scripts themselves.

LOOKING AT THE ENVIRONMENT

How is a selected area of the room or yard being used by children? Over a period of days or weeks, does anyone look at books or choose puzzles or build with blocks? If not, should that activity be put away for a while? Or, if the teacher thinks it's important, can she think of a way to reorganize it or move it or add other materials to it, to provide the attraction of novelty and to increase clarity and complexity? Could she develop a curriculum theme that might stimulate children's interest in those materials?

Out of observation comes action. The teacher in the following episode began with a management problem, observed carefully in order to understand a child's needs, and came up with an idea for play that she knew she would enjoy and predicted the children would too. She's an experienced teacher and her predictions are often sound.

> At Second Street preschool, sand play among the younger children has recently been characterized by throwing rather than purposeful digging or building. Mohammed, a particularly high-energy 3-year-old, repeatedly tries the adults' patience; they have been tempted to forbid him access to the sand in his more excitable moments. But there's so much sand, and so much to be learned by playing in it, that instead the teacher has invented a new play script that she hopes will make digging more interesting.
>
> On a day when both the aide and an experienced parent volunteer are available to supervise indoor play, the teacher invites a small group of children to come outside with her. "Let's sit at the table so you can see my book," she says. It's a story about a missing dinosaur bone. She shows them the pictures for a few minutes, then asks if they'd like to look for the missing bone. "I think we should try the sand," she says, handing out spoons for digging. There are tools in the sand too, and Mohammed replaces his spoon with a large scoop, with which he digs vigorously. And there are bones to be found in the sand—chicken bones, which the teacher had buried earlier in the day.
>
> BEN: We're using our muscles.
> MOHAMMED (*showing the teacher the muscle in his arm*): Big muscles.
> TEACHER: Good—the better to dig bones with!
> Mohammed tosses sand and gets it in his hair. He complains.
> TEACHER: Mohammed, you have to be careful. When you're archeologists you have to dig carefully.
> Sarah gets in Mohammed's way. He hits her with his scoop.
> TEACHER: Mohammed, you can't hit your friends.
> Clearly, they *are* friends. They're talking together eagerly. Mohammed shows Sarah his muscle. He digs vigorously.
> TEACHER: Think you've just about found all the bones?
> MOHAMMED: No, not yet. Digging, digging. I found a bone! (*All the children are digging. Mohammed tosses sand out of the box.*)

TEACHER: Remember, Mohammed, not so high.

He makes a concerted effort to toss the sand lower. He is enjoying the large muscle action which the dig-and-toss sequence provides. He experiments with a smooth swinging movement which sends the sand out in a lovely arc.

MOHAMMED (*digging hard again*): I found another bone!

SARAH: I found a little bone. I'm the bone collector.

BEN (*to Sarah, who is tossing sand*): Are you making a hole, Sarah?

MOHAMMED: Stop! Don't get sand on me.

SARAH: Gimme my spoon.

MOHAMMED: That's not your spoon, that's my spoon.

SARAH (*grabbing*): That's mine!

MOHAMMED: No, I want it back! (*He is now crying loudly.*)

TEACHER: Find any more bones lately?

MOHAMMED (*stopping his crying as abruptly as he started*): No.

SARAH: Teacher, I smell a bone in here.

TEACHER: You smell a bone? (*She begins digging, and Mohammed helps her.*)

SARAH: Yeah, Mohammed, we find all the bones, right? It's a baby bone.

TEACHER: We have to dig carefully. There's a baby one in the sandbox.

SARAH (*talking to Ben and Mohammed about their bone collection*): We gonna cook them.

TEACHER: When you cook them, what will you have?

SARAH: Chicken.

TEACHER: Oh, you start with bones, you get chicken?

SARAH: Yeah.

"The children do know they're chicken bones, don't they?" said the aide, who had come outside in time to overhear this thought.

"Yes, they know. But they had fun pretending to look for dinosaur bones. And so did I," said the teacher. "The children may not really care about archeology, but it makes the activity more fun for me. And when I'm having fun, I have more patience with kids who throw sand. I've also been noticing that Mohammed doesn't do it to bother people. He's using those big muscles—and I saw him really watching the movement of sand through the air."

This play was sustained for a full hour. Working in a small space, 3-year-olds encounter frequent problems of territory, which their teacher helps them solve. Problem solving is an important part of their work at this "dig." And these diggers are passionate about their work, as young children should be.

NAMING CHILDREN'S PLAY SCRIPTS

What scripts are children playing? A teacher might decide to keep a list of those she overhears or chooses to watch in action. How varied are they? Which children play which scripts? Are they sexist? Are there any scripts she might like to try to introduce, to broaden children's repertoire?

How much detailed knowledge of their scripts do children show? What do they know about procedures in medical settings, about the sequence of cooking a meal, about the behavior of airplanes? How rich is their vocabulary? Observation can be used to give a teacher ideas for adding props and new language to children's play, within the script they have established. By doing so, she can see if they are ready for more details and a "thicker" plot.

> At Live Oak preschool, for several days the baby doll has been bottle-fed. Today the teacher asks, "Is your baby old enough for baby food?" Camilla thinks about it. "No, she wants her bottle." She burps the baby and puts her to bed. The teacher retreats. But 2 days later, Camilla says suddenly, "Now she's old enough." The teacher has forgotten. "Who is?" "My baby," says Camilla impatiently. "She wants baby food."
>
> Children certainly know what they want when they want it, thinks the teacher delightedly, as she goes to the shelf where she has stored several baby food containers. "Here you are. There's peaches, and cereal, and strained peas. Can you find a spoon?" Yes, Camilla can. She puts the baby in the high chair, the teacher looks for and finds a bib, and a new scene has been added to the play.

> Fernando's driving script seems to be titled "Crash!" and the teacher is beginning to be concerned about the sturdiness of the bike he is riding. As he picks himself up for the fifth time she moves toward him. "You really crashed," she acknowledges. He grins. "This is my crash car." "Does your daddy crash his car too?" she asks. "One time he did," says Fernando. "Where were you?" asks the teacher. "Mom and me were in the backseat," says Fernando. "That must have been scary," the teacher suggests. "Mom was scared," Fernando acknowledges. "And Papa said a lot of words. I wasn't scared."

"What happened to the car?" asks the teacher.

"Papa took it to the garage," says Fernando. "They fixed it."

"Does your crash car need to go to the garage?" asks the teacher.

That's a new idea for Fernando. He gets down on the ground to inspect the bike. "Yeah," he decides. "It needs to be hammered right here. See?"

Zach has been listening. "My uncle Bob fixes cars," he says.

"Does he have a hammer?" asks the teacher.

"Yes," says Zach. "A hammer, and a wrench, and a oil can."

"Do you think you could fix Fernando's crash car?" the teacher suggests.

Zach gets seriously down to look at it. Fernando shows him where it crashed. Zach gets a shovel from the sandbox to use for a wrench. They are working together on it as the teacher moves on, making a mental note to bring some real tools the next day and propose building a garage for fixing cars.

INTRODUCING A NEW THEME

What are children doing and saying in response to a curriculum theme that teachers have chosen to introduce? Was the choice of theme a good one? Does it hold children's interest? Is it generating new vocabulary and stimulating conversation? Are children adding their own ideas to our planning web?

Sue Bush, who teaches 3-year-olds at Willard Children's Center, loves gardens, but gardeners don't love snails. Children are fascinated by snails.

"So one night," explains Sue, "I flooded my garden, and later I went out with a flashlight and collected snails. There were dozens and dozens of them. I brought them to school and gave half of them to Joyce, for her 4-year-olds."

The snails are in a clear container on the science shelf, with half a dozen children clustered around. Sue is taping a large sheet of dark blue paper onto one of the work tables. All the children but Alison, who is sponging the snack table, crowd around as Sue tips the snails out of their container onto the paper. They start making snail trails and climbing on each other—and on the children who want to hold them. There are plenty of snails for all the children. As the children and snails explore each other, Sue describes what she observes.

Some of us just want to look at the snails.
They don't want to touch them.
Don't put a snail on anyone else if they don't like it.
Chris likes his snail to walk on his arm.
But don't put a snail on someone who doesn't.

As she talks and watches and listens, she is writing down children's
words. Already, she has pages of notes. Animals stimulate children's
language and observational skills, and sometimes fantasy.

CHRIS: Look, Sue, he's crying.

SUE: What's the matter with him?

CHRIS: He wants to get down. Here you go, snail.

Sue has decided to write down one child's snail talk each day. Yesterday she listened to Ernie. Today, on the wall above the science
table, are Ernie's words (see Figure 8.1).

Snails - Ernie

Do they bite?
They move slow.
I don't want to touch it.
I touch them.
They don't bite.
Yuck! That snail slobbered on me.
Yikes!
They won't bite.
I'm making him roll.
I pick him up and put him in my hand.
They're cold, Sue.
He's crawling on my hand.
Oh, they're fighting.

FIGURE 8.1. Ernie's Words about Snails

Although this is the second day with snails, they've lost none of their novelty. For a full 15 minutes all the children are absorbed in snail watching and experimenting: What will he do if I put him here? While most of the children gradually go on to other activities, a few remain with the snails for 40 minutes. Ernie moves from the snails only as far as his teacher's note pad; he leans against her to watch her writing, then gets a pencil for himself and adds his own letter-like shapes among hers. She lets him, looking on with interest. When she finally lays down the pad to put the snails away, Ernie promptly picks it up. "See my O's?" he says to Chris.

In Joyce's room next door, the 4-year-olds, who have watched the snails laying down their silvery trails, are making "snail trails" of their own on paper, using food coloring in medicine droppers. Audrey gets markers and draws a page full of snails. She talks excitedly to her teacher, and Joyce writes her words: "Audrey made 17 snails." At group time, as the children keep talking about snails, Joyce shows them how she writes "snail" in English and "*caracol*" in Spanish.

When the two classes come together at outside time, Joyce shows Sue what Audrey has just spontaneously written on a piece of paper:

SNAIL
CARACOL
AUDREY
AUDREY

Joyce and Sue agree: "This theme is working!" Not like the gold-fish, Joyce remarks; we had six, and now there's only one, and no one seems to care. Snails, on the other hand, are stimulating absorbed exploration, of themselves, of oral language, and of the written word. The children are excited, and so are the teachers.

An arriving visitor is enthusiastically welcomed: "You've got to see this!" The visitor shares the teachers' enthusiasm, admires all the drawing and writing, and has a chance to play with the snails too. Tentatively, she reminds them of another mode of teacher play, one that had been discussed at a recent inservice: "webbing" as a way to plan and represent curriculum themes. They remember, and they're eager to try it.

Sure enough, the next time she visits, a web is posted on the wall in Joyce's room (see Figure 8.2).

"How did you do it?" the visitor asks.

"We weren't sure how we were supposed to do it, so we just sat

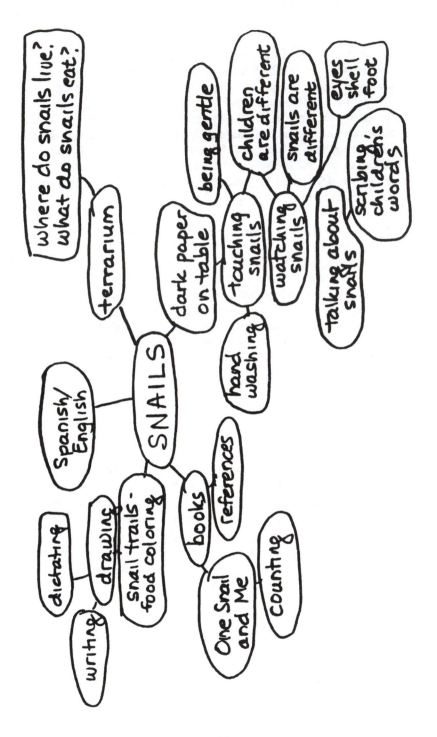

where do snails live?
what do snails eat?

terrarium

being gentle

children are different

snails are different

eyes
shell
foot

scribing children's words

dark paper on table

touching snails

watching snails

talking about snails

SNAILS

Spanish/ English

hand washing

books

references

dictating

drawing

Snail trails - food coloring

writing

One Snail and Me

Counting

down together during nap time with a big piece of paper. I wrote "SNAILS" in the middle of it," says Sue.

"And then we looked at each other and laughed. We didn't know what to write next," Joyce says. "So we decided to put down everything we had done to begin with and then add the things that happened along the way."

The visitor is a bit puzzled. "Can you show me?" she asks.

"Okay, look," says Sue. "We got out a terrarium to put the snails in so they wouldn't crawl all over the room. The kids all came around to see, and someone asked why I was putting them in there, and someone else asked where I got them, and we ended up in a long conversation about where snails live. I mentioned that I don't like them living in my garden because they eat my plants, and Chris wanted to know what they would eat at school, and I showed them the lettuce I had put in the terrarium. Since then I've seen children saving bits of food from snack and lunch to see if the snails will like it."

"I wanted a related art activity, and so I made up snail trails," Joyce explains. "The children have used droppers with food coloring before, and they enjoy them. This was a new name for the activity, which really stimulated several children's interest. And then Audrey went on to drawing and writing; she's just turned 5, and she's really into writing. Her mother is so pleased."

"I hadn't thought of any snail books, but they loved *One Snail and Me*" (McLeod, 1961), says Sue. "So do I. Thank you for sending it to us; we've been reading it over and over. Do you want it back today?"

"Oh no, keep it as long as you're using it," says the visitor. "And I saw another book on the table, too—a reference book on mollusks, I think?"

"Yes, I found that on my brother-in-law's bookshelves. The kids like the pictures a lot; they're mostly of ocean snails, and so they've started talking about the ocean. I guess it will soon be time to bring my SCUBA gear again." Sue is a SCUBA diver, and the ocean is a theme she regularly shares with children in her classes.

The visitor looks at the web some more. "I'm glad you included 'being gentle' and 'snails are different' and 'children are different,'" she says. "Those are certainly the things I heard you saying to the children, Sue, when they were handling the snails: 'Some of us like to touch snails, and some of us don't. There are big snails and little snails.' Nice."

Sue agrees. "It has been nice. Hand washing has been an outcome I certainly didn't think about at the beginning, but it's right there as something we talk about. Children and adults both get tired of remembering to wash hands, day after day, when there's no obvious reason for it. Snail slime is a fine obvious reason! And we all get to say 'Yuck' together as we scrub it off, but also to talk about why it's not yucky for the snails. They need that slime to keep from hurting themselves when they slide across rough places. The kids love that idea, even as they love saying 'Yuck.'"

"So have all the children gotten into snails?" asks the visitor.

"Not Evan," says Joyce. "Evan is my dinosaur boy. Let me show you his latest wonderful drawing."

The dinosaurs were indeed wonderful, and Joyce had put no pressure on Evan to give up dinosaurs because she was "doing snails." Themes in preschool are open-ended; like open-structure materials and teacher-established order in the material environment, they're suggestions, not the only way to go. Whole-class themes come both from teachers' ideas and from some children's questions and initiative. Those children whose initiative is directed elsewhere need support in continuing to develop their own ideas, in play and in other symbolic activities. The teacher's intent is to generate enough ideas to catch the interest of all the children, diverse individuals that they are. She wants each child to discover the things that sustain his or her real interest, not to put aside personal passions for what we're all studying now. Sustained group projects in which everyone is expected to participate are more appropriate to the later developmental stage of industry than to the preschooler's task of developing initiative (Erikson, 1950; Katz & Chard, 1989).

The web that the visitor encouraged the teachers to write down already existed in their heads as an invisible "web" of their own good ideas and their observations of children. Past their initial uncertainty in the face of a novel task, Sue and Joyce found it easy to make their ideas visible on paper. They aren't sure what to do with it next. Neither is the visitor, so they talk some more.

"Since you put up the web, has anyone noticed it?"

"Audrey has," says Joyce. "She recognized SNAILS, and then she asked me to read her the rest of it. I tried to read it to everyone at group time too, but some of the children got too wiggly. Snails are great, but these 4-year-olds aren't ready for all those words. You know what Kaylin and Nancy did, though? They started copying the web, ignoring the words. Mrs. Serrano, my aide, walked by and asked 'Is that a spider web? Where's the spider?' and Nancy said 'Make us a spider, please please,' and Mrs. Serrano did. (I have tried to get her to stop drawing for the children, but she couldn't resist that please please!) It worked out fine, though, because they decided they wanted lots of baby spiders and began copying the big one and ended up with a great variety of their own creation."

"So you could add spiders to the snail web, couldn't you? And Sue could think about adding ocean. Have any parents asked what you were doing?" The visitor is curious.

"No—but I've got it at the back of the room, and they don't usually come that far. That's an idea. I think I'll move it to the sign-in area and see if anyone comments," says Joyce.

"We put the web in Joyce's room because her kids are older," explains Sue. "When I put up words, most of the threes don't notice them, unless it's their own names. Except Ernie—you saw him writing all over my note pad. He showed his mom the 'Snails—Ernie' words I put up near the terrarium, and she read them to him again. When my kids pay attention to writing it's usually to me *doing* it, not to the words once they're done."

"Interesting. And that makes sense," says the visitor, "because most young children aren't yet ready for reading as a real task. What they do with reading and writing is just what they do with all the other adult behaviors they observe. They *play* them."

PLANNING FOR LITERACY AS A PLAY SCRIPT

Where adults model reading and writing, at home and at pre-school, children play reading and writing. Like other adult real-life behaviors, these behaviors have predictable scripts that children learn best by practicing them in their play. To read a book to a child, an adult chooses it from the shelf, holds it right side up, opens it from the front, turns the pages one by one, shows the pictures, and says the words. This sequence is obvious to an experienced reader, but young children are just learning it.

To encourage reading-as-play, a teacher models reading—to the group of children and, when possible, to one or two children on her lap or snuggled close. She makes the books—the same books she reads to the children—readily available to children during play time. She permits books to be taken to different parts of the indoor and outdoor environment. There are books and magazines and catalogs in several different areas—next to the doll bed to be read at bedtime, in a kitchen cupboard as pretend cookbooks, in the "office" for looking up important information, in a cozy area with pillows and stuffed animals where a child can relax and read to herself, her friend, her bear, or even her teacher. Like adult readers, children playing at being readers need control over a variety of reading materials, with which they are free to settle down wherever they are comfortable.

To encourage writing-as-play, a teacher models writing as a way to communicate messages and remember obligations, in all the ways communication is called for naturally in the life of a classroom. He writes notes to parents, planning lists, lists for turns, "PLEASE SAVE" signs, and names on paintings. He calls casual attention to the fact that he is writing, and he uses large, clear print whenever practicable. He invites interested children to "write" for all these purposes too, conveying his confidence in their ability to do so.

He thinks about the real-life settings in which people write and re-creates some of them in the play environment, stocking them with the tools people write with. And so there are pencils and pads of paper by the telephone, and a pad with a pencil on a string on the kitchen wall. He adds a receipt book and pens to the tools for fixing passing tricycles along the bike path, and next to the cash register in the store. There might be a doctor's office with prescription pads and patient charts, or a post office with envelopes and stamps and a mail box, or an office like this one at Second Street preschool.

> The teacher has just reorganized one corner of the room as an office, with two typewriters on a table, staplers and two telephones on a small desk, and, in the desk drawers, pens and pencils, used envelopes, and several small spiral notebooks. Luz and Yolanda discover the office with delight; a volunteer mother puts paper in the typewriter for Luz. "*Voy a trabajar,*" Yolanda announces. She picks up the phone. "Rrring, rrring. Hello, hello . . . *la señorita.* Okay. *Ahorita . . . voy,* okay? Bye."
>
> Another girl arrives. Yolanda and Luz tell her to go away, and she does. They continue their private conversation. Two other, smaller girls want to play in the office; "No! You can't come in here," says Yolanda, pushing her hands toward their faces. Holding hands, the little girls go to appeal to the teacher; seeing them go, Yolanda and Luz hide behind the table, yelling. The little girls do not return, and they come out again.
>
> Animal crackers and juice have been put out on a nearby table for children who are interested in snack. Yolanda goes out for a plate of animal crackers; she brings them to the office. Sarah arrives and is accepted; she types and talks on the phone. Luz relaxes with the animal crackers, putting her feet up on a chair. Yolanda looks for a wastebasket and Sarah goes to find one, getting the teacher's permission to take it to the office. Yolanda is writing in a notebook; she

tears out a couple of pages so Luz can write too. Then they get on the phone. Apparently it's a message go go out: Yolanda gets her jacket, calls "¡*Ándale, ándale!*" and out of the office they go, giggling with the excitement of the play. As they run around the room, the teacher calls, "*Sonando el teléfono,*" and back they go to answer the phone.

Luz and Sarah go off to the house area. Master player Yolanda follows her teacher's example: "¡*El teléfono—anda rápido!*" she calls, and back they come. Then all three are off again, this time to rescue the baby from a house on fire; several other children join the fire fighting, squirting pretend water. (They had recently gone on a class trip to the fire station.) When the excitement is over and it's clean-up time, Yolanda spends a long time putting everything away in its place, even lining up the typewriter carriage so it's just so.

As in much of real life, writing may be just one of the events in a complex play sequence. This office play included writing in a notebook and typing, coffee break, telephoning, and "This is Our Private Office" and "Emergency" scripts, interweaving ideas, props, and people from several areas of the room. The teacher's planning set the stage; she permitted movement of people and things from one area to the other, intervening within the script (by suggesting that the phone was ringing) to forestall running around the room. The children built on the teacher's play ideas by introducing their own. Everyone was creatively involved in the emergencies of meaningful curriculum.

PLAY-DEBRIEF-REPLAY

In play, we can try new things to see what will happen. In her book *Serious Players in the Primary Classroom* (1990), Selma Wasserman describes primary children's open-ended investigations of materials guided by teachers in a process she calls play-debrief-replay. The sequence is structured by the questions: What can you find out about this? (play) What happened? (debrief) Now what can you find out about this? (replay).

Play and *replay* are hands-on action and interaction with materials and other children. *Debrief* is conversation with the teacher and other children, which in the primary grades is sometimes carried on with the whole class. In many respects the process is like Paley's informal conversations with small groups of 3- to 5-year-olds about their play (1984, 1986a, 1988).

This model, we believe, can also be used by the teacher of young children in reflecting on her own process of emergent curriculum planning. In setting the stage, she is playing. What can I find out about the children if I get the bikes out, add water to the sand, put books next to the doll bed, increase the colors at the easel? In trying out new roles, she is playing. What can I find out if I ask children questions rather than putting them in time-out, if I join play as a visitor who has come to tea, if I draw a picture of a block construction and show it to the builder?

In reflecting on what she has found out, she is debriefing. What happened? she asks herself and, if she is fortunate, others. Adults, like children, learn more if they debrief in conversation with others. In this book we have given examples of several such conversations (see Chapters 2, 5, and 7, as well as this chapter) carried on among students with a master teacher and between a visiting observer and a teacher or two.

Inventing a snails curriculum, Sue and Joyce shared their ideas and observations with each other. They were aware from the beginning that it offered possibilities for hands-on science exploration, developing caring attitudes toward living things, and stimulating conversation. But it hadn't occurred to Joyce that snails could make their own colored trails. (That was a child's idea; she dropped food coloring on her paper and then got a snail to put in the color. Other children quickly noticed, and a whole new activity was born.) Nor had Joyce realized the extent to which her writing children's words would stimulate some children to practice writing for themselves. Sue had guessed that snails would interest the children but had not predicted that their interest would be sustained for more than a month, or that 3-year-olds might be interested in the act of writing. Making such discoveries along the way, teachers add to a curriculum web, modify a week's and, indeed, a year's plan, and keep observing, debriefing, and replaying. Just as the children do.

Teacher educators are among the people who engage in debriefings with teachers. They would be well-advised to follow Wasserman's and Paley's guidelines for asking genuine rather than loaded questions, which lead teachers "to think and say more about their problems and possibilities," instead of giving answers that close the subject (Paley, 1986b, pp. 124-125). To help teachers understand what is happening and why, a supervisor may paraphrase teachers' words or ask them to dig more deeply, engaging their thinking through responses that are respectful, attentive, and empowering (Wasserman, 1990). Adults learn complex tasks like teaching "in much the same way as young children learn—through experimenting, problem-solving, talking with peers, asking questions, and making mistakes and reflecting on them" (Carter & Jones, 1990, pp. 28–29).

In trying out more ideas to support play and challenge children's thinking, the teacher is replaying: Now what can I find out? Through this process the curriculum keeps emerging and the teacher, together with the children, keeps learning.

⑨ Paying Attention to Play

How much attention do playing children need? All children in group settings need a stage manager—an adult attentive to the order and contents of the physical environment. Children's need for the direct involvement of an adult as player or mediator, however, decreases as their own ability to sustain play increases. The teacher of master players has less need to *do*, and more freedom to observe and plan, than the teacher of beginning players.

SUPPORTING CHILDREN WHO HAVE NOT YET MASTERED PLAY

It isn't easy to pay attention to some children, those who have mastered, not play, but staying "invisible" (Rabiroff & Prescott, 1978). They need help in taking initiative, but often they remain unnoticed during play times—even though they may get considerable direct help at other times of the day.

At Second Street child care center, Becky, whom we first met in Chapter 1, is notably immature among the 4-year-olds. At planning time her teacher focuses clearly on her to help her say and do the expected things: "Tell me where you're going to play. Can you say it louder so I can hear? Good!" At transitions the teacher often speaks Becky's name to remind her of the next task to be accomplished. She's thoughtful about paying attention to Becky outside of play time.

During play time most of the 4-year-olds in this class are assertive and full of play ideas; it would be hard for the adults to miss what they're doing. "Teacher, look!" is frequently heard, as the children make sure their play is being noticed and appreciated. Their play scripts are full of action: We're Galloping on Our Horses, It's Vanessa's Birthday and She's Five, Superman to the Rescue. Surrounded by all this action, teachers of 4-year-olds may get out of the habit of noticing and responding to small beginnings, which the adults working with young 3-year-olds next door do all the time.

Here is Becky outside one day.

Stephanie and Vanessa are busy in the sand. Becky wanders in their direction, carrying a pail and shovel. As she steps into the sand the girls run off. She sees a dump truck and settles down with it, using her shovel to fill it with dirt. After a while she gets up, holding the truck, and turns it sideways to drive it along the whole length of the vertical wall. Then she drives it back to the sand, where Richard is now playing.

Becky plunks down in front of Richard, saying something softly. She digs a shovelful of sand and holds it up at an angle, watching the sand slowly run out of it. She watches Richard pouring sand into a funnel. She tries to take the funnel but Richard holds on; neither of them says anything.

Becky finds the dump truck again and starts driving it, this time along the narrow concrete edge of the sand area. She moves behind the swings, where two adults are pushing children. One of them is counting as she pushes. Becky stands up, holding her truck. "Look, wheels. One, two, three, four," she says softly. No one hears her.

Clean-up time is announced. "Becky, let's go," says the aide, taking her by the hand in a friendly way.

Becky tried a few small beginnings that might have developed into shared play scripts if anyone had helped. I'm Driving My Truck, How Can I Pour Sand?, One Two Three Four Wheels—rudimentary ideas, certainly, but they have possibilities. But the adults were occupied; the refrain, "Teacher, push me," is hard to ignore. It's important, though, to divide adult energy between response to children's requests and noticing those children who haven't learned how to ask for what they need.

The teacher was quick to acknowledge, when asked by an observer, that Becky was a child who needed special attention during play time. On another visit, the observer saw the teacher sit down in the sand near Becky, who welcomed the opportunity to ask a question about her teacher's recent absence and then started finding rocks for her: Two baby rocks. One big rock. The teacher was appreciative, and together they found a whole family of rocks.

On this occasion, no other children were nearby. On the earlier day, an attentive adult might have been able to initiate social play by taking on the role of mediator, stage manager, or player—perhaps like this.

Teacher as Mediator. Had an adult been nearer the sand, she might have offered assistance when Becky tried unsuccessfully to take the funnel. "Becky, you would like the funnel. Richard, you have a funnel. Becky would like a funnel too. What do you think we could do about that?" Depending on various factors, including Richard's willingness or unwillingness to share, the availability of extra funnels, and the adult's ideas for complicating play, parallel or cooperative dramatic play might have been an outcome of this intervention, giving Becky a place in the play life of the group.

Teacher as Stage Manager. Adults, with less at stake in play, can remain more alert than children to all the resources of the environment. Looking quickly around, an adult might have spotted an extra funnel, two cups, and several pails. Gathering them up, she could sit in the sand near Becky and Richard. "I found another funnel. Becky, would you like a funnel? I found some cups, too. Richard, do you need a cup? Becky, do you need a cup? What else do you need to pour sand?" By adding materials and including both children in her offer of them, an adult can suggest the possibility of playing together while adding the reassurance of her presence.

Teacher as Player. An adult can offer props and leave their use up to children, or can model their use as well. This adult, having found more sand toys, might have refrained from comment and simply settled down close to the children to play with them. She would respond to any show of interest with willingness to share. She might pour with one cup while putting the other cup strategically between herself and Becky. By her actions as well as her presence, she highlights the possibilities of sand play and invites social interaction and pretending: "Would you like a drink of my chocolate milk?"

It is at least as important to respond to children's initiative in play as it is to reinforce their desired behaviors in other situations. Mohammed's teacher, in Chapter 8, sometimes has difficulty finding desired behaviors to reinforce for him, but she manages to acknowledge all his play discoveries even while fending off his intrusions into others' space. Mohammed, of course, is a very visible child, guaranteeing himself adult response of some kind. Becky is one of the quiet ones, capable of making herself invisible.

SUPPORTING MASTER PLAYERS

Adults interested in the scripts children play find it easy to pay attention to master players. They're the children whose words delight our ears, whose skill in negotiation enables them to sustain play without our help, whose creativity in dealing with fantasy, friendship, and fairness—that trilogy of preschool priorities (Paley, 1986b)—reassures us that we are, after all, good teachers of young children. For nearly an hour one day, these 4-year-old master players placed no demands on their teacher; he was free to enjoy, to observe, and to write down some of their memorable words to share later with parents and other staff.

> Outdoors at Live Oak child care center a split-level water table—homemade, with cutout holes to insert plastic dishtubs—has been filled with cornstarch. Extra bowls, spoons, and trowels are at hand. Paula, Dena, and Megan are busy mixing; they have added leaves and dirt to the cornstarch.
>
> PAULA (*stirring competently*): We're making chocolate.
> DENA (*bringing more dirt*): This is chocolate. Stir it up.
> PAULA: We're making cookies and cream.
> DENA: Ice cream. Please can I have a cone?
>
> She presents a funnel to Paula, who fills it generously. Someone adds water to the mixture. "Don't," Paula yells, and the child, intimidated, retreats. Dena has finished her ice cream. Now she arrives with a cup of water to add to her friend's mixture.
>
> DENA (*dumping water*): Dumping. Lots of goosh.
> PAULA: No more. It's getting too gooey, right? We have a magic. We're magic witches of the East, right? She's never gonna learn about us. She'll die.
> MEGAN (*arriving*): We'll be the fairest one in the world. (*She starts stirring in the other tub.*)
> DENA (*running back and forth between the two tubs, with handfuls of mixture for each*): We're gonna have our magic. This is our magic food for Snow White.
> MEGAN: We don't blow hair out of our nose. The witch doesn't blow hair out of her nose. How about, we don't blow hair out of our nose, but our mother does?

When master players make messes with cornstarch and leaves, dirt and water, they aren't messes, they're magic potions or ice cream. Like the real cooks they watch at home, who magically transform raw materials into edible food, master players are remaking the natural world. Transformation, making something into something else, is a basic theme in both science and mythology. Transformation has particular importance for preoperational young children who, Piaget has told us, are still learning that a person or a thing can have more than one attribute at the same time. Transformations are the key to understanding reversibility, a necessary step in mastering arithmetic (Labinowicz, 1980). They are a key to literacy as well.

A teacher who knows something about this theory is reassured, watching these children at play: They're really learning something, they're not "just playing." They are thriving in the learning environment he has prepared for them. He can use his observations to reassure their parents, too, explaining why this play is developmentally important. Master players free a teacher to move into the roles of scribe, assessor, and communicator—appreciating children's skills in play and language and representing these on paper to be communicated to the other adults who have particular interest in these children's growth, and to the children themselves.

Teacher as Scribe. Taking notes as he watched this play, the teacher knew that these older 4-year-olds were becoming actively interested in reading and writing, and guessed that they might respond to a "chalk talk" about their play.

Because snack at Live Oak is a choice in the middle of play time, children don't all arrive or leave at once. Predictably, Megan, Dena, and Paula arrived together. The teacher had moved an easel near the snack table, and as they ate, he began to draw. They were immediately interested. "That's our water table," said Megan, as it took shape on the paper. "Who's that?" (see Figure 9.1a).

"Who do you think it is?" asked the teacher as he kept drawing.

"It's not me," said Megan decidedly. "My hair is real long. That silly person's got no hair!"

"It's Dena," teased Paula.

"It's not!" screamed Dena.

"Shall I give it some hair?" said the teacher, adding lots. "Now who could it be?"

Conversation continued as the teacher finished drawing people and began to write words (see Figure 9.1b). "That says Paula," announced Paula, proudly. "You wrote my name. What does that say?"

The drawing stayed on the easel, generating interest from other children as well as return visits from the girls to read names, add features to the figures, and make drawings of their own on new sheets of paper. The play itself resumed after snack, with elaboration of the Snow White theme and "lots of goosh." Imaginative language often grows out of messing for the sheer joy of it; both are open-ended, spontaneous explorations of unlimited possibilities.

Paula said, "We're making chocolate."
Paula said, "We're making cookies and cream."
Dena said, "We're making ice cream."
Dena said, "We're making goosh."
Dena said, "We're making magic food for Snow White."
Megan said, "We'll be the fairest one in the world."

FIGURE 9.1. "Who Do You Think It Is?"

Teacher as Assessor and Communicator. The chalk talk conversation enabled the teacher to make an informal assessment of each child's interest and skills in literacy. He noted that all three girls could read their own and each other's names, and were interested in the other words on the paper. Megan promptly recognized the water table; later in the day, she included it in a drawing of her own, surrounded by long-haired girls. Paula covered a page with her name, accurately printed. Dena's rainbow painting had *D*'s and *e*'s flying in its sky. "That's a *D*," she said to no one in particular. Then she looked at it again, attached another *D*, and added antennae and spots to make it into a butterfly. The teacher, as interested in creative thinking as he is in literacy development, made a note of that too and showed it to Dena's father at the end of the day. The girls spontaneously showed their parents both the teacher's drawing and their own, and communication flourished. "What did you do at school today?" Here it is!

Teacher as Planner. As an adult enjoys children's imaginativeness, he can be imaginative, too, in the role of planner. Are there ways in which he might extend and further enrich this already rich play by choosing an idea from it that sparks *his* thinking or by adding materials, conversation, storytelling, or the written word? How about adding cedar shavings or beach pebbles in the water table? How about making real chocolate or real ice cream or cookies? How about transforming the chalk talk into a flannel board activity that children could repeat on their own?

This teacher got excited by his flannel board idea. He cut out child-shapes in several shades of brown, tan, and peach to match the varied colors of the children in the class. He cut out a couple of water tables, a climber, swings on a frame, six bikes, several tables, and chairs. He added additional scraps that looked to him like nothing in particular but would probably look like something to children. He decided to tell a flannel board story about children playing outside, make the materials available during free play time, and see what happened. Watching his master players and responding to their ideas and demands, a teacher becomes a master player too.

TEACHER ROLE DEVELOPMENT

Like children at play, adults who work with children grow in their mastery of role behaviors. Developmentally oriented teacher education offers many opportunities to practice these roles and reflect on one's performance. But many staff members in preschool and kindergarten programs begin their work without such practice. Some of them have been trained in elementary education, which does not value play. Others bring goodwill and life experience but little training; their competence is based on past experience with children (including parenting) or on being in touch with the child in themselves (Jones, 1984, p. 185). On a teaching team they can contribute different perspectives. For example, grandmothers-become-caregivers often bring home-management skills to the larger stage of the preschool; drawing on these skills, they get satisfaction from creating clear figure–ground relationships and activity "menus" to serve to children in the form of crafts. Some young adults trying out child care as an entry-level job are especially good players; they can be encouraged to provision imaginatively for play as well as participate in it.

Stage manager is the most basic of the roles, to be mastered by all staff. In a well-ordered, well-provisioned environment with plenty of time for play, most children will be able to create and sustain their own play as they have always done in homes and neighborhoods. Play in itself meets many of young children's growth needs. It is a self-teaching, self-healing process.

Fortunately, stage management seems to be the easiest role to learn. Nearly all adults are experienced in organizing and maintaining living spaces and time schedules for themselves; this experience transfers directly to the preschool. And it is easier and more appropriate to learn to manipulate environments rather than to manipulate children. If things aren't going well, let's think about how we could move the furniture, change the schedule, add props for play, rethink our organization of learning centers (Greenman, 1988; Kritchevsky & Prescott, 1969). We can criticize how the stage set works without criticizing how the adults or children act. Working behind the scenes, we can experiment with space, time, and materials without having to change our interactions with children during the time we're on stage. Sensibly, developmentally oriented early childhood curricula begin with the concrete, hands-on arrangement of space and materials (Dodge, 1988; Hohmann, Banet, & Weikart, 1979).

Mediator, a necessary role if children are to grow in problem-solving skills, employs power *for* rather than power *on*. It is unfamiliar to many adults, who bring to children's conflicts either an inclination to withdraw from their expression of strong feelings, or a no-nonsense power *on* approach: "I'm the grown-up here and you do as I say." To help children find their own solutions rather than impose an adult solution seems to undermine some adults' sense of order, authority, and the rightness of things. They would rather teach obedience than critical thinking.

Power *on* solutions have the virtue of familiarity, for many children, and security; it is clear that this grown-up knows and enforces the rules. But such solutions, unlike those mediated with children, interrupt play and the development of autonomy. Mediation skills can be discussed, modeled, and practiced within the context of program policy that defines conflict resolution as a goal. They are not difficult to learn for those who believe in their importance (Muhlstein, 1990).

Player is a role that comes naturally to adults in touch with the child in themselves. In families, adults play with children in a variety of ways: conversation, roughhousing, make-believe, games with rules, storytelling, spontaneous games (Segal & Adcock, 1981). Such mutual play builds relationships and contributes to children's play skills as well.

We have, however, observed many thoughtful teachers who remain on the periphery of children's play, paying attention but not participating. Some of them, when asked, explain that they simply aren't comfortable playing with children. Others have made a deliberate choice based on their feeling that adult involvement undermines the initiative of children at play. As we discussed in Chapter 4, the age of the children and their familiarity with the culture of the preschool both seem to be significant considerations here; thoughtful adults intervene more readily in the play of children for whom the preschool or kindergarten is a new and unfamiliar place. They move toward the periphery as children become masters of play in this setting. Player is a useful but not necessary role, we have come to believe. Adults can share play ideas with children through props and conversation as well as through playing themselves.

Scribe, an unfamiliar role to many preschool teachers, seems nonetheless to be a welcome one, especially for adults who fail to see much value in "just playing" and who are invested in their "teaching" role. We have watched a teacher assistant whose special joy is in the adult-directed craft activities she meticulously prepares, as she discovers that writing down the children's talk about their work can provide impressive content for her beautiful bulletin boards. While she is busy writing, the children have more freedom to create without her help. Adults often find it easier to write down children's answers to questions asked at group time or to record their dictated stories than to capture their language during play; the latter task requires a more sophisticated observer. But the role definition, "teachers are people who write down children's words," seems generally to be a congenial one.

If elementary-trained or untrained staff assume the roles of *assessor*, *communicator*, and *planner*, they are likely to fall back on familiar versions of the school game. It is through direct teaching and questioning—"today we're learning the letter *B*"—rather than planning for and observing play, that many teachers keep themselves accountable. Accountability is important. But in early childhood programs, it is accountability *for play* that matters.

A PLACE IN THE WORLD FOR CHILDREN

Because play is self-sustaining, competent adult performances in the roles of stage manager and mediator will sustain a nurturing environment for young children in the short run. However, all the roles become important when teachers assume the care and education of young children over the long run. They are working in partnership with parents, who are already involved in the same roles at home.

Good parents assume these roles intuitively because they are invested in their child (Katz, 1980). They repeat her cute sayings to Grandma, take her picture and put it in the family album, and show her how to write the name they call her by. They plan family activities that include her, and special events for her because she's special to them. They are observant of her growth in competence because they are invested in her accomplishments as mirrors of their success in parenting. For *personal* reasons rooted in the meaning of their life as a family, parents document and plan for their child's growth, giving her and themselves a firm sense of their shared past and future. She is theirs, and what she does matters very much to them.

Professionals are motivated not by their love for a particular child but by their skills and commitment to the importance of developmentally appropriate experiences for all children (Katz, 1980). A child in an early childhood program is a member of a group of children that has no permanence, no past and future, and in which he is no longer so special. While a few programs admirably attempt to compensate for this impermanence by keeping a group of children together with the same adults for several years, or by other variants of "family grouping," the realities of staff and family mobility create frequent separations and losses.

Professional rather than personal responsibility provides the continuity in children's experience in early childhood programs. Children becoming master players are occupied in representing, in order to understand, the continuing stories of their own lives. Under the conditions of modern society, most children need help from adults in doing so. In traditional societies the play of young children often has been ignored by adults, and children have been let be—typically under conditions of adequate space and time, availability of natural materials, and a wide-age community of children for whom the observable work and ceremonial world of adults is a ready source of play themes. In such a setting the stage for children's play is set by the community as a whole, and play is facilitated by adults' leaving it alone.

In some homes and neighborhoods, similar play conditions can be found even in modern society. But increasingly they have become the exception rather than the rule. And so we have teachers and other specialized caregivers responsible for the daily lives of many children under school age and faced with defining suitable roles for adult behavior in preschool group settings. Further, children and adults alike are living in a diverse, complex, and rapidly changing world in which the ability to define and solve new problems is a crucial skill to be developed. It is no longer enough for young children to imitate the behavior of their elders in order to grow up competent.

When parents care for children at home they have many other tasks to accomplish as well, thus ensuring children some freedom from constant supervision. In out-of-home child care settings the adults are constrained, often legally, to watch children every minute in order to be responsible for their safety. Simply "minding" young children, while doing nothing else of importance, is a task that fails to challenge the competence or sense of duty of most responsible adults. And so they look for other roles. Of these the most familiar, acquired through their own school experience, is teacher-as-teller—someone who gives information and orders to (hopefully) quiet and obedient children. True, some adults find themselves engaged in frequent struggles with noisy and innovative children, but these struggles help to justify the importance of their work; they are establishing civilized order in the face of primitive chaos. Teacher-as-disciplinarian is another familiar role that goes with the territory in schools.

All the roles we have described in this book are less familiar. They reflect modern theoretical views, rather than traditional commonsense views, of how children learn. They are, for the most part, professional rather than technical roles, requiring continual exercise of judgment rather than mere carrying out of standardized, trainable procedures. These roles call for skills in dramaturgy, mediation, observation, assessment, and creative planning. They ask adults to take the play of young children seriously, while being playfully responsive to its unfolding.

Parents' competence in child rearing comes directly out of the relationship: Because this child is mine, I will do my very best for her. This motivation for competence is largely absent in people caring for other people's children in groups. A popular alternative approach to competence, reflecting behaviorist thinking, has been to try to train caregivers as technicians. "Teacher-proof curricula" comparable to those that pervade elementary education (in spite of the professional certification of elementary teachers, as Kamii, 1985a, has pointed out) can be found in abundance on the display tables at any early childhood conference.

For several reasons, we believe this approach to be inadequate. One reason is the very limitation of training opportunities and the rapid turnover of child care workers. Technical knowledge takes time to acquire. A second, more significant reason reflects a point made by Jean Baker Miller (1976)—that there are tasks (historically, these are usually women's tasks) that are too variable to be approached technically. Like the high-level professions, they require the continual exercise of judgment. One such task is child rearing.

Third, as Nel Noddings (1984) has described, the ethical imperative underlying both child rearing and early childhood education is *caring*. Adults who choose to work with young children are, for the most part, people who enjoy children and who believe, on the basis of their own positive or negative experience, that the quality of childhood matters. In this experience lies the source of the empathy that is essential to caring and that supports an appreciation of the importance of play in the lives of young children. Young children at play are happy and lively, qualities such adults appreciate. The creation of a community of caring people, big and little, is the most important goal in child care. People who care about each other help each other grow and learn (New, 1990).

The early childhood professionals on a program staff or in supervisory positions are present to model all the teacher's roles, while taking primary responsibility for assessing, communicating, and planning. In most programs they provide leadership to a staff team with varying levels of experience and training (NAEYC, 1990). We believe that the best advice they can give to all staff is, *try not to interrupt play*. It will make most sense if the advice giver is on the spot while children are playing, to name the play, describe it in detail, and represent it for both adults and children in a variety of ways that enable the adults to slow down, pay attention, and appreciate the importance of children's learning through play.

10 A Sense of the Past and the Future

Play is not simply a tool that adults can manipulate to hurry children toward "school readiness." Although Piagetian theory has given a solid cognitive response to the question, "What is play good for?" children undertake play for its own sake. Play is the natural activity of early childhood—what children do best.

Monighan-Nourot (1990), reviewing the historical development of rationales for play in early childhood education, distinguishes between the philosophical/moral rationale, which "rests on the belief in the inherent value of the childhood activity of play in and of itself and represents a humanistic attitude in protecting the rights of the vulnerable and malleable child," and the instrumental rationale, which demands evidence that play has future value for the child and society (p. 60). Instrumental justifications abound, she comments, "in the research literature generated by Piagetian notions of the contribution of play to development" (p. 77). In our view, looking at the place of play in a developmental sequence, as we have done in Chapter 1, offers more than instrumental justification for children's play. Development is a history, a story; the human life cycle is a pattern, a narrative in which each chapter has its own significance and each player discovers her own play.

> In the days when the Eldest Magician was getting Things ready, he told all the Animals that they could come out and play. And the Animals said, "O Eldest Magician, what shall we play at?" and he said, "I will show you." He took the Elephant—All-the-Elephant-there-was—and said, "Play at being an Elephant," and All-the-Elephant-there-was played. He took the Beaver—All-the-Beaver-there-was—and said, "Play at being a Beaver," and All-the-Beaver-there-was played. (Kipling, 1902/1978, pp. 143–144)

Children play at being a Child. Their play is a form of representation; it is one of the necessary stages in a developmental sequence. Looking at behavior developmentally gives it a past and a future. Children are learners as well as doers. What they're learning by playing is mastery of play, an important mode of being in the world, which will serve them all their lives as well as here and now (Csikszentmihalyi, 1975).

THE LOGIC OF HUMAN RELATIONSHIPS

Most educators, even in early childhood, are more interested in teaching their adult ways of thinking about the world to children than in exploring the child's own meanings. Professionals in any field are apt to behave in this way, striving to teach the student or client the professional's language rather than to learn the language of the other (Watzlawick, Weakland, & Fisch, 1974).

Children's meanings are embedded in their experiences. But as Margaret Donaldson (1978) has pointed out, our technological society places the highest value on the capacity for *disembedded* thinking. "The better you are at tackling problems without having to be sustained by human sense the more likely you are to succeed in our educational system" (pp. 77–78). Disembedded thinking is objective,

> abstracted from all basic purposes and feelings and endeavors. It is totally cold-blooded. In the veins of 3-year-olds, the blood still runs warm.
>
> This is in no way to suggest that the ability to deal, in cold blood, with problems of an abstract and formal nature is unimportant. It is immensely important. Much that is distinctly human and highly to be valued depends upon it. And young children are bad at it. (Donaldson, 1978, pp. 17–18).

Before they can become good at it, however, they need to put first things first—to learn about "basic human purposes and feelings and endeavors." The play in which young children invest so much of their cognitive and affective energy is not primarily concerned with problems of an abstract and formal nature, with the classification of colors, numbers, and spatial relationships. Imaginative play is the medium that, according to Vygotsky (1978), frees young children's embedded knowing. It is the arena where children are no longer bound by the immediate perception of things and come to rely instead on the expression of symbolic meanings. Imaginative play is "the zone of proximal development" where children can perform "a head taller" than they are capable of under normal circumstances because the context is appropriate to childhood forms of knowing.

Young children's primary concern is *human* relationships. Daddy, mommy, sister, and baby are understood before bigger, big, little, and littlest. Home, an emotionally laden image, is understood before house, a building where people live together. Children's play integrates feelings and facts; it is both art and science.

> The classroom has all the elements of theater, and the observant, self-examining teacher will not need a drama critic to uncover character, plot and meaning. We are, all of us, the actors trying to find the meaning of the scenes in which we find ourselves. The scripts are not yet fully written, so we must listen with curiosity and great care to the main characters who are, of course, the children. (Paley, 1986b, p. 131)

Play can best be understood through skilled teachers' stories of children's play and conversations about play (Clemens, 1983; Griffin, 1982; F. Hawkins, 1974; Paley, 1984, 1986a, 1988, 1990). As Coles (1989) and Egan (1989) insist, stories are often more effective conveyors of human knowledge than scientific analyses are.

> We need, for the educational benefit of children, to reconstruct our curricula and teaching methods in light of a richer image of the child as an imaginative as well as a logico-mathematical thinker. What we call imagination is also a tool for learning—in the early years perhaps the most energetic and powerful one. (Egan, 1989, p. 17)

In their accounts of children's apparent "illogic," sensitive observers uncover the emotional logic of their stories and dramatic play.

> "Frederick, I'm curious about something I heard you say in the doll corner yesterday. You said your mother doesn't have birthdays any more." (Frederick knows my tendency to begin informal conversations in this manner, and he responds immediately).
> "She doesn't. How I know is no one comes to her birthday and she doesn't make the cake."
> "Do you mean she doesn't have a birthday *party*?"
> "No. She really doesn't have a *birthday*."
> "Does she still get older every year?"
> "I think so. You know how much old she is? Twenty-two."
> "Maybe you and your dad could make her a birthday party."
> "But they never remember her birthday and when it's her birthday they forget when her birthday comes, and when her birthday comes they forget how old she is because they never put any candles. So how can we say how she is old?"
> "The candles tell you how old someone is?"
> "You can't be old if you don't have candles."

"Frederick, I'll tell you a good thing to do. Ask mother to have a cake and candles. Then she'll tell you when her birthday is."

"No. Because, see, she doesn't have a mother so she doesn't have a birthday."

"You think because your grandma died your mother won't have any more birthdays?"

"Right. Because, see, my grandma borned her once upon a time. Then she told her about her birthday. Then every time she had a birthday my grandma told. So she knew how many candles to be old." (Paley, 1986b, p. 125)

This is a competent 4-year-old, figuring out the world. Is it any wonder that, as Paley (1986b) says, "'Birthday' is a curriculum in itself" (p. 126), which someone in the group plays out every day? By listening for the "answers I could not myself invent" (p. 125), Paley opens windows for herself and her readers into the meaning-filled worlds of the preschool child and offers a model for other teachers having conversations with children.

Some proponents of cognitively oriented curriculum claim that these meaning-full worlds are inaccessible to adults. "It's easier and more productive to focus directly on, say, children's planning than on group dynamics, on classifying objects and events than on interpreting fantasies—the one is concrete and intelligible, the other abstract and esoteric" (Hohmann, Banet, & Weikart, 1979, p. 1). Teachers who believe that fantasies are more abstract than classification of objects regularly interrupt children's dramatic play scripts with their own agendas (see Chapter 5). Play is storytelling. It is both concrete and intelligible to adults who take the trouble to "learn the language of the other"—the playing child. A teacher who has taken a great deal of trouble to learn this language explains, "'Pretend' often confuses the adult, but it is the child's real and serious world, the stage upon which any identity is possible and secret thoughts can be safely revealed" (Paley, 1990, p. 7). Young children's greatest strength in the acquisition of knowledge is their passion for play.

Teachers who have faith in the process of development can capitalize on it, building on developmental strengths rather than reacting to deficiencies. We are not simply advocating the maturationist, "leave them alone to grow" view that Kohlberg (DeVries & Kohlberg, 1990) has labeled *romantic*. As we have made clear throughout this book, teachers have important roles in children's play. Growth is an interactive process. Children learn through adult guidance as well as through their self-directed encounters with the world. Such guidance, we believe, should be directed toward the mutual creation of an adult–child culture in which meanings are shared.

STORIES, IMAGES, AND THE CREATION
OF CULTURE

The bridge from embedded toward disembedded thinking is best built through stories and images rather than through abstractions. Bridge building should begin with the child's personal concerns, a beginning that asks the teacher to use power *with* rather than the consistent power *for* of the cognitively oriented teacher (see Chapter 5). As observer, player, and asker-of-questions, the power-*with* teacher looks and listens for the "answers I could not myself invent" (Paley, 1986b, p. 125), for the "key words" and images that, unlike the "key experiences" abstracted from Piagetian theory (Hohmann, Banet, & Weikart, 1979), erupt from the volcano of the child's emotionally laden experiences (Ashton-Warner, 1963).

Cognitive theory and practice give priority to the development of logical reasoning, viewing intuition and the arts as precursors to logical and scientific thought. Psychodynamic theory, which recognizes the threats that anxiety introduces into the growth process (Erikson, 1950; Maslow, 1962), supports a view of the arts as creative, complementary modes of thought that serve adults as well as children (DeVries & Kohlberg, 1990). The arts create the power of magic, essential for dealing with the things that go bump in the night. All cultures use magic in the face of the unknown. The arts, in the hands of both children and teachers, provide the creative vent for the child's volcanic energy (Ashton-Warner, 1963). Teachers of young children can support children's play by becoming *keepers of metaphor*—both source and recorder of stories and images.

In all cultures, people who share experiences create metaphors—stories, song, dances, and visual images—in order to remember their experiences, given them new meanings, and build community through their sharing. Among the several basic needs of young children, one is a *sense of the past and the future* (Jones & Prescott, 1982). Children need to know that they have a place in the world, that they matter, and that they will be cared for. Families convey this knowledge through stories and images: "When you were a baby . . ." "When Mommy was a little girl . . ." "When we go to Grandmas, we'll . . ." "When it's your birthday. . . ." Photographs are taken, passed around, and talked about. Great-grandma crocheted that afghan; Uncle Bud built that table.

People who live together need to create a culture together, in order to make connections with each other and assure themselves that their time together is of value. Even preschool children in day care are occupied with creating a peer culture, often focused on the stories and images from their common experience with entertainment media: TV, video, and movies. For older children, peer culture that adults may find offensive supports the process of growth toward independence. But 3-, 4-, and 5-year-olds aren't ready for independence; they need adults to take care of them and to share meanings with. Young children's takeover of media dramas more appropriate for older children distances them from adults too soon, in a society in which children leave home for day care younger and younger and are thus physically distanced from the people with whom their deepest meanings are shared.

TEACHER AS KEEPER OF METAPHOR

The ways in which teachers and caregivers can establish metaphoric connections with young children include (1) joining their media play, (2) introducing alternative dramatic scripts, and (3) representing children's stories, images, and play in new modes.

Joining Children's Media Play

I explained to the children that I wanted to understand more about why children like to play Teenage Mutant Ninja Turtles and chase games. I announced that I would be interviewing them individually with a tape recorder . . . I had 30 volunteers the first day!

I responded with curiosity and openness to the many "lessons" the children gave me. I watched the television show and conversed with the children about past episodes. Interestingly, the children's active play seemed to change almost immediately after I shared my interest in "Turtle Culture." They no longer took on a clandestine manner as they chased each other on the playground. Instead, they yelled to me as they ran past, "Jacob is Shredder and we're all Donatello chasing him!" I could then respond in the correct lingo, "Cowabunga, Dude!"

The aggressiveness of the play lessened. As I watched more closely, I saw that most of the kicking and karate-chopping was indeed an attempt at "fake fighting." Unfortunately, the amount of necessary skill in controlling such gross motor movements is not well developed in kinder-

garten, so injuries did occur. With the advent of the Ninja Turtles movie, I
was able to introduce the concept of stunt men and women who practice
very carefully planned fake fights. A simple reminder of "Fight like they
did in the movie" was all that was needed most of the time. (Gronlund,
1990, p. 3)

Gronlund's experiment with her kindergarten class, undertaken
out of her concern that "their play did not appear imaginative, rich, or
inventive to me" (p. 1), followed the suggestion of Carlsson-Paige and
Levin (1987) that adults can respond to, challenge, and complicate
children's war and weapons play. The children's eagerness to include
an interested teacher suggests that they do not seek to be left on their
own with media stereotypes; it is our distaste that leaves them there.
This teacher's willingness to exercise power *with* gave her access to the
peer culture and thus expanded her opportunities to teach.

Introducing Alternative Dramatic Scripts

I begin by telling the story over several times. Very quickly most children
pick up the progression and begin to join the chorus of "Who's that trip-
trapping over my bridge?" "It's me, the littlest Billy Goat Gruff."
      When the children are all familiar with the structure of the tale, I ask
if they would like to act it out. There is an immediate wave of "I want to
be _____." I explain that we will act the play many times until everyone
has had a chance to play all the parts he wants. (Howarth, 1988, pp. 160–
161)

Howarth (1988, 1989) introduces fairy tale dramatization into the
classroom as an alternative to the "hard, indigestible, violent stereotypes, particularly male" that are children's diet in the mass media.
Fairy tales have historical rather than commercial roots; they have
stood the test of time. They are found in all cultures, and the tales
selected by a teacher should make connections with the family cultures of the children in her class, as well as broadening children's
experience through familiarity with tales from other heritages.
      "As in all great dramas, the themes in fairy tales echo humanity's
deepest concerns and fears, thereby facilitating each child's growth
and development" (Howarth, 1988, p. 173). They expose children to
the "'archetypal images we all need to confront," offering potential
situations and characters to be incorporated into children's playing out
of the issues in their own lives. These issues are not all easy ones; good
and evil are present in children's lives, even the best of them.

We do not limit the colors we offer them with which to paint; we encourage their experimentation with art media, enriching their environments with texture and shape. But we are often afraid to recognize that a child's life is made up of both light and dark feelings, which she also needs to name and utilize. How can she know that humankind has experienced all these same feelings for millennia? (Howarth, 1988, p. 162)

Stories told and books read to young children should be more than factual; they should be dramatically memorable, with potential for being played, talked about, assimilated into one's own language. "Who's that trip-trapping over my bridge?" said the great big Troll. "You monkeys, you. You give me back my caps" (Slobodkina, 1947). But Pierre said, "I don't care" (Sendak, 1962).

Representing Children's Stories, Images, and Play in New Modes

"Once upon a time," said Joan to her small class of 3-year-olds, whom she had called into a snug circle as their "going camping" play was coming to an end, and before clean-up time, "there were one, two, three, four, five, six, seven, eight children who went camping together." "Me!" said Charlie excitedly. "Me too!" said Alicia, echoed by others. "Yes, Charlie, and Alicia, and Mark went camping," acknowledged Joan, going on to name every child. "They put their sleeping bags in the car, and they put their tent in the car, and they put their food in the car. Then they put all themselves in the car, and they drove and drove until they got to the camping place. "In the mountains," explained Mark. "In the mountains," agreed Joan. "They got out of the car . . ." "I got out of the car," said Alicia. "Alicia got out of the car, and Paul got out of the car, and everybody got out of the car. They took their tent out of the car, and they put it up. They put their sleeping bags in the tent. They cooked their dinner." "On the fire," said Charlie. "They cooked their dinner on the fire and they ate it all up. They went to sleep in their sleeping bags. In the morning they got up and they cooked their breakfast and ate it all up. . . . And after they were all through camping, they put everything in the car, and they cleaned up every bit of their campsite, and that was the end."

Joan Newcomb, who teaches at The Little School in Bellevue, Washington, is telling children a story about themselves in the same way that families do. In conversation she cites Newson and Newson's

(1976) claim that storytelling about their children is one of the most important aspects of good parenting.

> The child is dependent cn his parents' role as a memory bank to which he can continually refer for evidence of himself as an individual with a history. One of the means by which the ordinary child achieves a sense of personal identity is through his store of memories going back into his own past. . . . It must be remembered that the child does not maintain this store of memories on his own, but has them repaired, added to and embroidered upon in everyday conversation with his own family. (p. 404)

Looking back in her teaching, Joan remembers a home visit.

> Everyone, including the siblings, had a humorous story to relate about the youngest child, Forrest, who was in my class. "Remember the time Forrest hid the peas from dinner in his diaper?" Forrest even joined in telling stories about himself. It was obviously a well-developed family sport. It gave me the feeling that this family had a special quality I can only describe as glueyness. (Newcomb, personal communication, 1990)

What is the "glue" that brings a family, or a class, together? Joan as storyteller is re-creating the play of the 3-year-olds, using her words to involve them in the making of a communal art form. The children have invented and played their version of the story; some of them were eager to retell it with her. Others listened. If they're interested, she'll tell it again on another day: "Remember when you all went camping?" inviting memory of past events and creating a shared tradition that builds group cohesion—a sense of the "we" who do memorable things together.

Joan also adds artifacts to some of her stories, introducing objects with which the children were playing: "And the last time anybody saw that ghost, she was wearing this exact same hood." Becoming a prop in a story elevates a familiar object to a new level, Joan says. It becomes in great demand in the play that follows.

Because these children are 3-year-olds, the teacher's retelling is oral, with liberal use of gestures and props. By the time they're 4 or 5, some of the children will also be interested in written words, which have their own sorts of rhythm on the page.

> We all went camping.
> Charlie went camping.

Alicia went camping.
Mark went camping.
Paul went camping.
We all went camping yesterday.

FROM HERE AND NOW TO THERE AND THEN: BUILDING BRIDGES OF MEANING

Oral and written retelling of children's play is an approach we described in Chapter 6. We have also given examples of teacher drawings of children's play activities and constructions—another mode of retelling, with images. Vivian Paley has invented still another approach to retelling: guided dramatization by children of their dictated stories (Paley, 1981).

All these approaches make a direct transition into language-experience and whole-language approaches to teaching literacy to older children. If Joan had in fact written the children's camping story, she would have had a language-experience chart (Van Allen, 1976; Veatch, Sawicki, Elliott, Barnette, & Blakey, 1973). The patterned language of memorable stories can not only be shared in storytelling but also discovered in Big Books (Holdaway, 1979). Children can "write" as well as dictate their stories, inventing writing for themselves in the process (Harris, 1988; Heigl, 1988). Children simultaneously talk, draw, and write their own stories (Dyson, 1989). Words that loom large in importance in children's play and stories can be written for them to copy and expand into written stories (Ashton-Warner, 1963; Clemens, 1983; Johnson, 1987). Curriculum themes introduced by the teacher can serve as an integrated focus within which all these activities can go on, building a shared classroom culture, just as John Dewey (1938, 1990/1943) proposed.

All these activities may begin in kindergarten or with older 4-year-olds and be fully implemented in the primary grades. All build bridges of meaning for children. Both in preschool and in primary, the teacher sustains and participates in children's creative process by inventing conscious, sustained responses to their stories and images. Teachers represent the child's words and images back to the child in ways that both affirm the meanings and model different ways in which meanings can be represented.

With 3- to 5-year-olds it seems to us particularly important that teachers represent for children not only their dictated stories but their *play*. Play is what young children do best; in play, they are at their most thoughtful and articulate, using body language as well as words. To represent children's play, the teacher must pay attention to it, noting the scripts children are playing and selecting the content to be recorded. In contrast, when taking dictation from a child while other children are playing, the teacher is ignoring the play. It is important, we believe, to pay attention to play.

In the High/Scope curriculum (Hohmann, Banet, & Weikart, 1979) children come together after play for *recall*, at which they are asked to talk about their play. In the oversimplified version often adopted by teachers, recall becomes a classification exercise. "Where did you play?" "I played in the block area." "Who did you play with?" "I played with Juanito." The richness of the play scripts, which included fantasy and feelings as well as mundane facts, is lost when young children are asked to talk, in a group, about the play they have already played.

Preschool teachers, Tizard and Hughes (1984) have found, ask children questions about their play—often questions to which they already know the answers, like those above. In contrast, the mothers in Tizard and Hughes's sample (both working class and middle class) discussed a wider range of topics with their children.

> At school, because the talk concerned play, it was almost alwayss concerned with the "here and now." At home, events outside the present context, including the child's own past and future, were more often discussed. . . . The school curriculum was, in fact, considerably narrower than the home's—a smaller range of topics was discussed. (p. 183)

Adult–child conversations at school were briefer than those at home and much more adult-dominated. "It was the staff who tended to keep the conservation going, and who did most of the talking" (Tizard & Hughes, 1984, p. 186).

The question, "Can you tell me about your play?" like the question, "Can you tell me about your painting?" implies that meaning can be communicated only through words—that drama and art need prose explanation. It is, in fact, a teacher-question, designed not to get real information but to stimulate oral language. Tizard and Hughes (1984) describe a conversation between a teacher and a child named Joyce; they then ask:

> Why are the teacher and child talking at all? Clearly it is not because Joyce has anything she wants to say to the teacher at this particular moment. Rather, the conversation is taking place because the teacher sees

an opportunity to introduce certain educational ideas (in this case, to do with size and shape) into the child's play. . . . Joyce does not respond with enthusiasm to this approach. (p. 191)

In a good home, children's play is not the focus of attention. In a good early childhood program, it is—because most of the people present are children and what they do together is play. The primary responsibility of the adults present is to facilitate play. But it is also their responsibility, we believe, to do what adults do much better than young children—to expand children's experience to include the there and then as well as the here and now.

Mothers in good homes ask questions to which they don't already know the answers, and they give information to children about matters of mutual interest (Tizard & Hughes, 1984). The parent–child relationship is a genuine and long-lasting one; information-giving thus includes stories about past and future events in the family's life. Quality early childhood programs take the family rather than the school as their model (Prescott, 1978). This implies both plenty of opportunities for informal adult–child conversations and, in the group, storytelling *by the adult* rather than recall or show-and-tell by the children.

Adult storytelling comes from books and traditional tales. It comes from trips we've taken together and events we're planning for next week. And it can come from a teacher's observations of the children, using her skills to recapture the scripts from their play, inviting but not requiring their participation in the retelling. (Teachers familiar with the call-and-response tradition characteristic of storytelling in some cultures may find ways to involve children in story participation just as they do in action songs, but with responses developed by the group members to fit their own story. "In the mountains," said Mark. "On the fire," said Charlie.)

The spontaneous play of young children is their highest achievement. In their play, children invent the world for themselves and create a place for themselves in it. They are re-creating their pasts and imagining their futures, while grounding themselves in the reality and fantasy of their lives here and now. Re-creating children's play in her own words, the teacher shows respect for its integrity, while building on it as one of the shared, recurrent experiences out of which the group's culture can grow. For this purpose, as well as for play's inherent value for children, teachers need to pay attention to play.

References

Ashton-Warner, S. (1963). *Teacher*. New York: Simon and Schuster.

Ballesteros, D. (1988). A language-enhancing classroom. In E. Jones (Ed.), *Reading, writing, and talking with four, five and six year olds* (pp. 129–135). Pasadena, CA: Pacific Oaks College.

Bereiter, C., & Engelmann, S. (1966). *Teaching disadvantaged children in the preschool*. Englewood Cliffs, NJ: Prentice-Hall.

Bissex, G. (1980). GNYS *at work: A child learns to write and read*. Cambridge, MA: Harvard University Press.

Bredekamp, S. (Ed.). (1987). *Developmentally appropriate practice in early childhood programs serving children from birth through age 8*. Washington, DC: National Association for the Education of Young Children.

Bredekamp, S. (Ed.). (1991). *Guidelines for appropriate curriculum content and assessment in programs serving children ages three through eight*. Washington, DC: National Association for the Education of Young Children.

Carlsson-Paige, N., & Levin, D. (1987). *The war play dilemma: Balancing needs and values in the early childhood classroom*. New York: Teachers College Press.

Carroll, L. (1979). *Alice's adventures in wonderland*. New York: Grosset & Dunlap. (Original work published 1899).

Carter, M., & Jones, E. (1990). The teacher as observer: The director as role model. *Child Care Information Exchange, 75*, 27–30.

Clemens, S. G. (1983). *The sun's not broken, a cloud's just in the way*. Mt. Rainier, MD: Gryphon House.

Coles, R. (1989). *The call of stories: Teaching and the moral imagination*. Boston: Houghton Mifflin.

Csikszentmihalyi, M. (1975). *Beyond boredom and anxiety: The experience of play in work and games*. San Francisco: Jossey-Bass.

Delpit, L. (1986). Skills and other dilemmas of a progressive black educator. *Harvard Educational Review, 56* (4), 379–385.

Delpit, L. (1988). The silenced dialogue: Power and pedagogy in educating other people's children. *Harvard Educational Review, 58* (3), 280–298.

Derman-Sparks, L., & A.B.C. Task Force. (1989). *Anti-bias curriculum*. Washington, DC: National Association for the Education of Young Children.

DeVries, R., & Kohlberg, L. (1990). *Constructivist early education: Overview and comparison with other programs*. Washington, DC: National Association for the Education of Young Children.

Dewey, J. (1938). *Experience and education*. New York: Macmillan.

Dewey, J. (1943). *The school and society*. New York: Macmillan. (Original work published 1900)

Dodge, D. T. (1988). *The creative curriculum for early childhood*. Washington, DC: Teaching Strategies, Inc.

Donaldson, M. (1978). *Children's minds*. Glasgow: Fontana/Collins.

Donmoyer, R. (1981). The politics of play: Ideological and organizational constraints on the inclusion of play experiences in the school curriculum. *Journal of Research and Development in Education, 14* (3), 11-18.

Duckworth, E. (1987). *"The having of wonderful ideas" and other essays on teaching and learning*. New York: Teachers College Press.

Dyson, A. H. (1989). *Multiple worlds of child writers: Friends learning to write*. New York: Teachers College Press.

Egan, K. (1989). *Teaching as storytelling*. Chicago: University of Chicago Press.

Elkind, D. (1989, October). Developmentally appropriate practice: Philosophical and practical implications. *Phi Delta Kappan*, pp. 113-117.

Erikson, E. (1950). *Childhood and society*. New York: Norton.

Ferreiro, E., & Teberosky, A. (1982). *Literacy before schooling*. Portsmouth, NH: Heinemann.

Franklin, M., & Biber, B. (1977). Psychological perspectives and early childhood education: Some relations between theory and practice. In L. Katz (Ed.), *Current topics in early childhood education: Vol. 1* (pp. 1-32). Norwood, NJ: Ablex.

Freire, P. (1970). *Pedagogy of the oppressed*. New York: Seabury.

Gonzalez-Mena, J., & Eyer, D. W. (1989). *Infants, toddlers, and caregivers*. Mountain View: CA: Mayfield.

Graves, D. (1983). *Writing: Teachers and children at work*. Portsmouth, NH: Heinemann.

Greenman, J. (1988). *Caring spaces, learning places: Children's environments that work*. Redmond, WA: Exchange.

Griffin, E. F. (1982). *Island of childhood: Education in the special world of the nursery school*. New York: Teachers College Press.

Gronlund, G. (1990). Exploring the war play dilemma in my kindergarten classroom (Occasional Paper). Pacific Oaks College, Pasadena, CA.

Harris, L. (1988). Journal writing at Pine Hill. In E. Jones (Ed.), *Reading, writing and talking with four, five and six years olds* (pp. 207-219). Pasadena, CA: Pacific Oaks College.

Harste, J., Woodward, V., & Burke, C. (1984). *Language stories and literacy lessons*. Portsmouth, NH: Heinemann.

Hawkins, D. (1974). *The informed vision: Essays on learning and human nature*. New York: Agathon Press.

Hawkins, F. P. (1974). *The logic of action*. New York: Pantheon Books.

Heath, S. B. (1983). *Ways with words: Language, life and work in communities and classrooms*. Cambridge: Cambridge University Press.

Heigl, J. (1988). Language experiences for language-delayed children. In E. Jones (Ed.), *Reading, writing and talking with four, five and six year olds* (pp. 121–128). Pasadena, CA: Pacific Oaks College.

Hohmann, M., Banet, B., & Weikart, D. P. (1979). *Young children in action: A manual for preschool educators.* Ypsilanti, MI: High/Scope.

Holdaway, D. (1979). *The foundations of literacy.* Portsmouth, NH: Heinemann.

Howarth, M. (1988). Fairy tale dramatics: An approach to oral language and personal meaning. In E. Jones (Ed.), *Reading, writing and talking with four, five and six year olds* (pp. 159–173). Pasadena, CA: Pacific Oaks College.

Howarth, M. (1989). Rediscovering the power of fairy tales: They help children understand their lives. *Young Children, 45* (1), 58–65.

Johnson, K. (1987). *Doing words.* Boston: Houghton Mifflin.

Jones, E. (1983). On the use of behavioral objectives in open education. In E. Jones (Ed.), *On the growing edge: Notes by college teachers making changes* (pp. 63–66). Pasadena, CA: Pacific Oaks College.

Jones, E. (1984). Training individuals: In the classroom and out. In J. T. Greenman & R. W. Fuqua (Eds.), *Making day care better: Training, evaluation, and the process of change* (pp. 185–201). New York: Teachers College Press.

Jones, E. (1987). Preparing children for a changing society: What *are* the basics? In *Pursuit of excellence in education: Beyond the basics* (pp. 173–204). Nashville: Tennessee State University.

Jones, E. (1990). Playing is my job. *Thrust for Educational Leadership, 20* (2), 10–13.

Jones, E., & Meade-Roberts, J. (1991). *Assessment through observation: A profile of developmental outcomes* (Occasional Paper). Pacific Oaks College, Pasadena, CA.

Jones, E., & Prescott, E. (1982). Day care: Short- or long-term solution? *Annals, 461,* 91–101.

Kamii, C. (1985a). Leading primary education toward excellence: Beyond worksheets and drill. *Young Children, 40* (6), 3–9.

Kamii, C. (1985b). *Young children reinvent arithmetic: Implications of Piaget's theory.* New York: Teachers College Press.

Kamii, C. (Ed.). (1990). *Achievement testing in the early grades: The games grown-ups play.* Washington, DC: National Association for the Education of Young Children.

Katz, L. G. (1980). Mothering and teaching: Some significant distinctions. In L. Katz et al. (Eds.), *Current topics in early childhood education: Vol. III* (pp. 47–63). Norwood, NJ: Ablex.

Katz, L. G., & Chard, S. (1989). *Engaging children's minds: The project approach.* Norwood, NJ: Ablex.

Kipling, R. (1978). *Just so stories.* New York: Weathervane Books. (Original work published 1902)

Kritchevsky, S., & Prescott, E. (1969). *Planning environments for young children: Physical space.* Washington, DC: National Association for the Education of Young Children.

Kuschner, D. (1989). Put your name on your painting but . . . the blocks go back on the shelves. *Young Children, 45* (1), 45–56.

Labinowicz, E. (1980). *The Piaget primer: Thinking, learning, teaching.* Menlo Park: CA: Addison Wesley.

Maslow, A. (1962). *Toward a psychology of being.* New York: Van Nostrand and Reinhold.

McLeod, E. W. (1961). *One snail and me.* Boston: Little Brown.

Meade-Roberts, J. (1988). It's *all* academic! In E. Jones (Ed.), *Reading, writing and talking with four, five and six year olds* (pp. 91–103). Pasadena, CA: Pacific Oaks College.

Miller, J. B. (1976). *Toward a new psychology of women.* Boston: Beacon Press.

Monighan-Nourot, P. (1990). The legacy of play in American early childhood education. In E. Klugman & S. Smilansky (Eds.), *Children's play and learning* (pp. 59–85). New York: Teachers College Press.

Muhlstein, E. (1990). *Facilitating social problem solving with children ages two through five* (Occasional Paper). Pacific Oaks College, Pasadena, CA.

National Association for the Education of Young Children. (1990). *Model of early childhood professional development* [draft]. Washington, DC: Author.

New, R. (1990). Excellent early education: A city in Italy has it. *Young Children, 45* (6), 4–10.

Newson, J., & Newson, E. (1976). *Seven years old in the home environment.* London: Allen and Unwin.

Nicholson, S. (1974). How not to cheat children: The theory of loose parts. In G. Coates (Ed.), *Alternate learning environments.* Stroudsberg, PA: Dowden, Hutchinson, and Ross.

Noddings, N. (1984). *Caring: A feminine approach to ethics and moral education.* Berkeley: University of California Press.

Paley, V. G. (1981). *Wally's stories.* Cambridge, MA: Harvard University Press.

Paley, V. G. (1984). *Boys and girls: Superheroes in the doll corner.* Chicago: University of Chicago Press.

Paley, V. G. (1986a). *Mollie is three: Growing up in school.* Chicago: University of Chicago Press.

Paley, V. G. (1986b). On listening to what the children say. *Harvard Educational Review, 56* (2), 122–131.

Paley, V. G. (1988). *Bad guys don't have birthdays: Fantasy play at four.* Chicago: University of Chicago Press.

Paley, V. G. (1990). *The boy who would be a helicopter: The uses of storytelling in the classroom.* Cambridge, MA: Harvard University Press.

Peterson, R., & Felton-Collins, V. (1986). *The Piaget handbook for teachers and parents.* New York: Teachers College Press.

Piaget, J. (1973). *To understand is to invent.* New York: Grossman.

Prescott, E. (1978). Is day care as good as a good home? *Young Children, 33* (2), 13–19.

Prescott, E., Jones, E., Kritchevsky, S., Milich, C., & Haselhoef, E. (1975). *Who thrives in group day care?* Pasadena, CA: Pacific Oaks College.

Rabiroff, B., & Prescott, E. (1978). The invisible child: Challenge to teacher attentiveness. In E. Jones (Ed.), *Joys and risks in teaching young children* (123–133). Pasadena, CA: Pacific Oaks College.

Reynolds, G. (1988). When I was little I used to play a lot. In E. Jones (Ed.), *Reading, writing and talking with four, five and six year olds* (pp. 85–90). Pasadena, CA: Pacific Oaks College.

Segal, M., & Adcock, D. (1981). *Just pretending: Ways to help children grow through imaginative play.* Englewood Cliffs, NJ: Prentice-Hall.

Sendak, M. (1962). *Pierre.* New York: Harper.

Slobodkina, E. (1947). *Caps for sale.* New York: Scott.

Smilansky, S. (1968). *The effects of sociodramatic play on disadvantaged preschool children.* New York: Wiley.

Smilansky, S., & Shefatya, L. (1990). *Facilitating play: A medium for promoting cognitive, socioemotional and academic development in young children.* Gaithersburg, MD: Psychosocial and Educational Publications.

Snow, C. E. (1983). Literacy and language: Relationships during the preschool years. *Harvard Educational Review, 53* (2), 165–189.

Solow, J. (1989). *Words through wonder.* Unpublished master's thesis, Pacific Oaks College, Pasadena, CA.

Sparrow, B. (1988). What really matters: The teacher in the concentrated encounter. In E. Jones (Ed.), *Reading, writing and talking with four, five and six year olds* (pp. 232–240). Pasadena, CA: Pacific Oaks College.

Stadler, S. (1990). *Layers of learning: Literacy for children and teachers.* Unpublished master's thesis, Pacific Oaks College, Pasadena, CA.

Stallibrass, A. (1989). *The self-respecting child: A study of children's play and development.* Reading, MA: Addison-Wesley.

Stritzel, K. (1989). *Blockbuilding and gender.* Unpublished master's thesis, Pacific Oaks College, Pasadena, CA.

Suransky, V. P. (1982). *The erosion of childhood.* Chicago: University of Chicago Press.

Tizard, B., & Hughes, M. (1984). *Young children learning: Talking and thinking at home and at school.* London: Fontana/Collins.

Toffler, A. (1980). *The third wave.* New York: Morrow.

Trook, E. (1983). Understanding teachers' use of power: A role-playing activity. In E. Jones (Ed.), *On the growing edge: Notes by college teachers making changes* (pp. 15–22). Pasadena, CA: Pacific Oaks College.

Van Allen, R. (1976). *Language experiences in communication.* Boston: Houghton Mifflin.

Van Hoorn, J., Nourot, P. M., Scales, B., & Alward, K. (in press). *Play at the center of the curriculum.* Columbus, OH: Merrill.

Veatch, J., Sawicki, F., Elliott, G., Barnette, E., & Blakey, J. (1973). *Key words to reading: The language experience approach begins*. Columbus, OH: Merrill.

Vygotsky, L. S. (1978). *Mind in society: The development of higher psychological processes*. Cambridge, MA: Harvard University Press.

Wasserman, S. (1990). *Serious players in the primary classroom*. New York: Teachers College Press.

Watzlawick, P., Weakland, J., & Fisch, R. (1974). *Change: Principles of problem formation and problem resolution*. New York: Norton.

Index

Metaphor, teachers as keepers of, 123–
127
in introducing alternative dramatic
scripts, 124–125
in joining children's media play, 123–
124
in representing children's stories,
images, and play in new modes,
125–127
Milich, C., 72
Miller, Jean Baker, 117
Monighan-Nourot, P., 118
Moralizing, power on, 50
Motor skills, 71
Muhlstein, E., 2, 114
Mumenschanz mime troupe, 89

National Association for the Education
of Young Children (NAEYC), 117
Negotiation
play as, 55
skills in, 108–109
New, R., 70, 85, 90, 117
Newcomb, Joan, 125–126
Newson, E., 125–126
Newson, J., 125–126
Nicholson, S., 23
Noddings, Nel, 117
Note-taking. *See* Scribes, teachers as
Nourot, P. M., 14
Nurturers, teachers as, 86

Observers, teachers as, 12–13
One Snail and Me (McLeod), 99
Open-ended scripts, 100
Order, maintenance of, 13
Outdoor play
half a class at a time, 77
picnics, 38–39
scripts to create power with
relationships in, 47–49
stage management for, 16, 20–23

Pacific Oaks College and Children's
School, ix
Painting, 77–80
Paley, Vivian G., 7, 30, 103–104, 109,
120–122, 127
Parents, xi
child rearing competence of, 117

communicating to, 78–83
note-taking and, 58
roles intuitively assumed by, 115
as skeptical about value of play, 87
Partnership Project, ix
Pasadena Unified School District, ix
Pearce, Ruth, vii
Perceptual skills, 16
Peterson, R., 2
Physical knowledge, 15
Piaget, Jean, 86, 109
cognitive development theory of, xi–
xii, 1–6, 118, 122
Picnics, 38–39
Piers, Maria, 7
Planners, teachers as, xii, 89–105
assessment and, 71–72
emergent curriculum and, 90–91, 104
in introducing new scripts, 95–101
of literacy as play scripts, 101–103
in looking at environment, 91–94
in naming children's play scripts, 94–95
in play-debrief-replay, 103–105
in supporting master players, 112
Play
boundary concerns of, viii
as bubble of illusion, vii
children's passion for, 121
content of, 9–10, 27–28
creating dichotomy between work
and, 86
instrumental rationale for, 118
as natural activity of early childhood,
118
in new modes, 125–127
paying attention to, 106–117
philosophical/moral rationale for, 118
prohibition of, 86
reasons for, xi–xii
requirements of, viii
as self-chosen, vii
as self-sustaining, 115
skepticism about value of, 86–87
Play-debrief-replay, 103–105
Players, teachers as, xiii, 34–42
in "Call Mikey," 34–35
in "Can X-Ray See This Lady?," 39–40
in "Don't Let the Babies Die," 35–36
goals of, 40–42
in interrupting play, 43

About the Authors

Elizabeth Jones is a member of the faculty in Human Development of Pacific Oaks College and Children's Programs in Pasadena, California, where she has taught both adults and children. She earned an M.A. in child development at the University of Wisconsin and a Ph.D. in sociology at the University of Southern California. She collaborated on Elizabeth Prescott's studies over a 10-year period on day care as a child-rearing environment; her recent studies have focused on teacher education and adult learning and on children's development of play, language, and literacy. She has been a visiting lecturer at the University of Alaska and in 1986 was DeLissa Fellow at South Australian College of Advanced Education. She is author of numerous articles and books, including *Dimensions of Teaching–Learning Environments* (1984) and *Teaching Adults: An Active-Learning Approach* (1986), and editor of *Reading, Writing and Talking with Four, Five and Six Year Olds* (1988).

Gretchen Reynolds is an adjunct faculty member at Pacific Oaks College in Pasadena, California, and an instructor in the early childhood education certification program at Algonquin College in Ottawa, Ontario, Canada. She has been an instructor in the teacher education program at the University of Alaska–Juneau, and has taught preschool and kindergarten children in Juneau and at the Pacific Oaks Children's School in Pasadena. She received an M.S. in Education from Bank Street College of Education in New York City. Her recently completed dissertation for the Ph.D. in Education from the Claremont Graduate School in Claremont, California, is titled *Behavioral Characteristics of Four-Year-Old Master Players*. She has authored several articles, including "When I was Little I Used to Play a Lot" in *Reading, Writing and Talking with Four, Five and Six Year Olds*, Elizabeth Jones (Ed.) (1988).